Gender

Qualities, Quirks, and Quarrels

Enhanced Edition

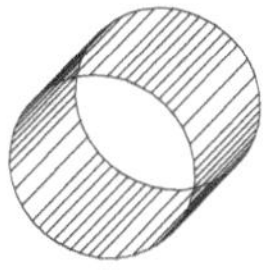

Author's Books

(As of June 20, 2020)[*]

Non-fiction

The Nature of Love and Relationships **2011, 2016**
Doubts and Decisions for Living:
  Volume I: The Foundation of Human Thoughts **2014**
  Volume II: The Sanctity of Human Spirit **2014**
  Volume III: The Structure of Human Life **2014**
Relationship Facts, Trends, and Choices **2016**
The Mysteries of Life, Love, and Happiness **2016**
Marriage and Divorce Hardships **2016**
Gender Qualities, Quirks, and Quarrels **2016**
Relationship Needs, Framework, and Models **2016**
Being Better Beings **2020**

Fiction

Persian Moons **2007, 2016**
Midnight Gate-opener **2011, 2016**
My Lousy Life Stories **2014**
Persian Suns **2021 (Planned)**

---

[*] 12 older books are Enhanced Editions and printed in 2020. They were resubmitted to the Library and Archives Canada Cataloguing as well. If a book's 'print date' on the copyright page is older, the newest version is available at Amazon and bookstores.

Love and Relationships Series
4

Gender

Qualities, Quirks, and Quarrels

(The War of Sexes)

Tom Omidi, Ph.D.

Love and Relationships Series # 4

Omidi, Tom, 1945-
Gender qualities, quirks, and quarrels : the war of sexes / Tom Omidi.

(Love and relationships series ; 4)
ISBN 978-1-988351-07-0 (paperback)

1. Sex (Psychology). 2. Sex differences (Psychology).
3. Interpersonal relations. 4. Man-woman relationships. I. Title.

Old edition at
Library and Archives Canada Cataloguing in Publication
BF692.2.O45 2016 155.3'3 C2016-902407-5

Published by Eros Books,
Vancouver, British Columbia
Canada

erosbooks2020.@gmail.com

Enhanced and Printed in 2020

Table of Contents

Table of Contents (Cont.)

INTRODUCTION

Human species is incredible in so many ways, including aptitude, attitude, logic, mentality, sentimentality, creativity, cruelty, etc. The multidimensionality of our character is just amazing, especially in the ways we combine these attributes so artfully often with no obvious consistency. All these special talents make our heads spin and wonder whether any aliens, even if they existed, could compete with humans in terms of the vast variety of attributes we enjoy.

A large multi-volume book about our qualities, quirks, and quarrels would be quite educational, entertaining, and sad in many respects. A few of those volumes only about 'human interactions' would be especially interesting. However, the matter becomes ten folds more perplexing when we explore gender encounters and differences. In particular, the prevalent disturbing effects of these differences in marital relationships make us question God's wisdom to create men and women so differently. Therefore, this topic is briefly tackled in this book. Naturally, people perceive events and people according to their unique personalities. However, it also appears that men and women have major, yet uniform, differences in terms of mentality, perceptions, priorities, and interpreting life.

We have personally felt the gender divergence in mentality and feelings, and history supports our observations, too. While genders' physical and hormonal differences are obvious, their behavioural and emotional differences have been a matter of curiosity, excitement, and irritation regularly, especially in the new era. Even more amazing, the more we have tried to study and practise gender equality, the more gender differences have manifested, and the more conflicts have risen between men and women.

Overall, as relationship conundrums increase in society, we feel both obliged and intrigued to study gender mentalities and answer questions like the followings:

1. Are gender differences significant enough to measure and validate?
2. What kinds of effects these differences have on people's lives and happiness?
3. How much of the differences are useful or harmful for both personal welfare and interacting with the opposite sex?
4. What is the importance of knowing these differences?
5. How much of the differences are genetics?
6. How much of the differences are related to cultural and lifestyle influences?
7. How much of the differences are the results of variations in genders' perceptions of the world and life?
8. Are increasing misperceptions about the purpose of life and lifestyles alienating genders?
9. Is the increasing shallowness of social values going to drive gender differences and conflicts to the extreme?
10. Are gender differences consistent around the globe or change due to culture and lifestyles?

This book would emphasize mainly on the first four questions to the extent our review might help relationships. In particular, the discussions in the following chapters about these questions lead to six main conclusions:

A. Men and women think, feel, and behave differently in general, although they usually follow the same logical and behavioural patterns.
B. While gender differences appear universal and studied for the overall population, they do not necessarily apply to all men or women. Plenty of exceptions exist regarding the general observations made in this book.
C. Gender differences make a substantial impact on couples' relationships both positively and negatively.
D. Gender differences are growing these days and they are mostly weakening the fundamentals of social structure, hinder teamwork in families, and reduce the chance of personal happiness.
E. At the same time, gender differences have the potential to enrich family life and social structure **IF** people learn how to apply their gender qualities (differences) in a teamwork atmosphere to create synergy at many levels.
F. The importance of knowing about gender differences is to increase couples' sensitivity about their symptoms, which they should face realistically, as inherent features of their relationships. In fact, this knowledge could help them take better advantage of those gender differences once they set their mindsets properly.

The assertions and analyses presented in this book are based on prevalent findings in social and psychological disciplines as well as the author's academic research explained under the heading of 'Personality Chart and Ratings' on page 172.

PART I

Gender Qualities

CHAPTER ONE
Human Personality

In order to understand gender differences, we must know a little bit about human personality in general. Then, we can study gender differences according to various dimensions of human personality. As a first step, we can signify and measure someone's personality in terms of how effectively he/she can:

a) apply his/her **instincts**,
b) reason and use his/her **logic**,
c) connect with people and society—**model**, and
d) manage his/her **ego** for his/her own benefit.

The above four personality factors reflect people's major urges to think, feel, and behave in certain ways:

- **Instincts** drive many of our urges starting from the basic urge for sex up to the complex urge for spirituality. This factor reflects the *inner self* of a person.
- **Model** drives our urges to socialize and adapt. This factor reflects the *social orientation* of a person and his/her need for compassion and acceptance.
- **Ego** drives our urges to defend ourselves and to push our desires on others. This factor reflects a person's *object*

orientation, i.e., greed and a need to succeed in acquiring objects or dominating them.

- **Logic** drives our urges for decision making and planning. It reflects our ability to use our brain and reason. This factor reflects the *goal orientation* of a person.

Most people use only a small portion of each of the above four factors in any situation to make their decisions, thus the quality of our actions and behaviour is normally substandard. Nevertheless, a person's personality manifests according to a combination of above four factors that s/he usually uses in his/her daily encounters and actions. Accordingly, the intensity of each factor in the mix makes a person's personality unique. These concepts are explained in more detail in the References at the end of the book and demonstrated in the Personality Chart on Page 172.

At the same time, a person with a *rather perfect* personality could *theoretically* make the best use of all four personality factors to fulfill his/her needs and goals. S/he can use his/her instincts, has great commonsense, knows how best to adapt to the environment, and applies his/her Ego in the most *effective manner*. The term 'Effective Manner' demands that a person's objectives are humanistic and not merely selfish. Many people can use their Ego and Model effectively for personal benefit only, e.g., our haughty politicians who manipulate the public for their own and their sponsors' benefits. However, for this book's intention at least, a rather perfect personality should acquire certain qualities that can make him/her a better human being overall, including the use of his/her Ego and Model.

Therefore, it becomes obvious that hardly anybody has a perfect, balanced character. We have our unique personalities, which reflect our strengths and weaknesses in terms of the personality factors that we have either inherited genetically or acquired in society. For example, a person with higher Model tendency is mostly emphasizing on socializing and adaptation, whereas a person with high Ego tendency is too self-centred and object oriented. A person could be considered normal, and not perfect, when s/he makes a rather balanced use of all his/her personality factors. Alas, most of us do not qualify even as a normal person due to our insecurities, quirks, and inadequate use of instincts and logic. We are mostly Model and Ego driven, which means we have very high social and/or object orientations, and are trapped in our obsessions for love, greed, and egoism.

Approximate ratings for human personalities, along the above noted four factors, are offered in the following pages based on a simple mechanism developed by the author. This mechanism provides a chance for making tentative estimates of gender and average personality ratings in modern societies. For interested readers and scholars, the background for these ratings, including a personality chart, is provided at the end of the book in the References.

The personality ratings offered in this book suggest that an average human in a modern society is only slightly driven by instincts (about 20% of all his/her instinctual capacities), he/she knows how to adapt to his/her environment by using Model (on about 70% of occasions), and he/she is highly self-centred and object-oriented (in about 80% of his/ her dealings with people), and he/she benefits from commonsense and logic to some extent (about 30% of his/her total potential). Thus, using the above noted percentages, we can say that an overall personality rating for humans is (20,70,80,30), which reflects their average capacity for using their instincts, model, ego, and logic respectively. This rating is obviously too far off the ideal personality that can be imagined for a rather perfect personality.

Gender Personality Ratings

Now, the fun part!

Men and women with all types of personality ratings are found anywhere on the wide personality spectrum (i.e. in the rectangle shown in the Chart on Page 175 in References). Yet, it seems safe to suggest the average ratings of (30,80,70,20) and (10,60,90,40) for women and men respectively. These two ratings are shown as 'Women' and 'Men' in the Chart.

These ratings reflect that women are depending more (compared to men) on their instincts for their decisions and actions (30% for women versus 10% for men). On the other hand, men depend more on their logic (20% for women versus 40% for men). Women's intuitiveness helps them in many ways as explained in this book. Mainly, it makes them more capable of applying their Model to their advantage in a natural way and adapt easier in social settings. Model makes women more charming than men (80% for women versus 60% for men). In addition, it helps them rebound after a relationship breakdown much better and faster. Use of their Instincts and Model also makes women more assertive and decisive. They also are better equipped to bond together more naturally and deeply than men do. Men are weaker in all these respects. Men are more aggressive because they are more Ego oriented than women (70% for women versus 90% for men). Overall, we can show the following ratings:

Instincts Model Ego Logic

Women : (30,80,70,20)
Men : (10,60,90,40)
Humans: (20,70,80,30)

The above comparative gender ratings, according to their level (percentage) of Instincts, Model, Ego, and Logic, are used in this book for discussing gender differences.

Gender differences in terms of people's use of four personality factors appear not significant on the surface, yet even these minor differences are affecting gender qualities and attitude noticeably. Even a fraction of one percent variation in any of the four personality factors, e.g., use of Ego, makes a major difference in a person's perceptions and behaviour. The effects and symptoms are not only vivid during our personal contacts, but also lead to major relationship conundrums and the rise in divorce rate. Of course, gender differences account only for a rather small portion of a person's personality. Family genetics and rearing environment affect people's personality much deeper than any other factor, including human hormones or any other cause for gender differences, e.g., the impact of new culture as noted below.

On the other hand, gender differences would most likely grow faster every decade, as culture and people's personal needs and tendencies change in line with their obsession for individualism and higher expectations from life. Social setting and people's shallow lifestyles affect the formation of people's unique personalities. Thus, gender differences would widen every decade and relationship conflicts grow, too. Of course, everybody would still hold all the four main dimensions of personality attributes, especially Ego, which its share would most likely continue to rise in both genders. Everybody is, in fact, getting more selfish and phony every year. Accordingly, this rising egoism would have deep repercussions for cultures and relationships, while its symptoms would widen gender differences that lead to less stable relationship environments and more family conflicts.

CHAPTER TWO
Gender Personality Attributes

Nature and nurture develop people's personalities in line with their genetics, gender, intelligence, outlook, rearing environment, and life experiences. Accordingly, people build personalities with unique qualities and quirks. Meanwhile, it seems that some personality attributes are clustered based on gender in interesting ways that indeed put men and women in some distinguishable classes.

Generally, we rely on our personality attributes to manage our lives, be assertive, and defend ourselves in our own ways, but then our differences have caused too many conflicts and clashes at all personal and social levels. Furthermore, all these unique personalities must somehow learn to come together in order to build functional societies and families. Indeed, finding practical means of teamwork has now become too urgent for humans' survival.

Ironically, gender differences could prove valuable if we address and align them properly. They can stir efficiency and synergy if couples learn to use them in a teamwork setting. In fact, these qualities are often so nicely complementary, we wonder if God or evolution has designed genders artfully just for couples' welfare through teamwork. Yet, nowadays, we sabotage nature's clever scheme. Humans just do not know how to mix their gender qualities to increase synergy in their relationships. Our modern mentality seems to be ruining the effect of natural evolution that aids all creatures. We refuse to grasp and enjoy God's divine intention for creating genders different! Instead, everybody insists on propagating some raw visions of equality and doing the same types of activities with intense rivalry. We strive for individualism and independence as if fully oblivious of our reasons for choosing to cohabit in societies and families and how much we need one another to survive. We imagine so arrogantly that our crude perception of individualism is accurate and can be easily aligned with social living requirements. We fuss and fight over equality naively, instead of benefiting our complementary qualities. Therefore, people's innate qualities often turn into quirks and nuisances for others, e.g., when confidence turns into cockiness.

Nevertheless, six fundamental facts about gender qualities and quirks are crucial to consider throughout this book:

1. People have much more common traits and quirks than differences. Common attributes, such as ambition, greed, and a large host of crooked personal needs discussed in Chapter 7 drive both genders rather equally. Accordingly, relationship frictions are more due to genders' common needs and traits than their personality differences.
2. Although genders' unique qualities and related symptoms annoy the opposite gender, without such disparity people would have damaged their relationships and tortured one another even more. Just imagine both genders being equally decisive and active mostly intuitively, or sloppy by nature. Not only more frictions would have erupted all the time between partners, but also their life routines would have become even tougher and riskier without at least some preliminary checks and balances that the existing gender differences impose on relationships.
3. Each gender quality and its symptoms are related to some other personality attributes (qualities and symptoms) for

that gender. For example, men's passivity is the outcome of their cautious mind, loose nature, realism, poor identity, laziness, etc. Thus, people cannot change their personality attributes readily even if they agreed on their destructive nature for them or their relationships.

4. A major challenge for couples is to learn how to apply their conflicting gender qualities effectively in order to stir synergy in their relationships and relate easier. This goal must eventually feel natural and logical to them in order to learn compromise and teamwork for fulfilling their marital purposes. Such smart respect of their conflicting qualities would be a tough challenge, of course, but essential for curbing their pomposity and dogmatism, especially about their gender identities and whimsical ideals.
5. As the first step for success in relationships, people and society must revamp their mentalities about the purposes and potentials of relationships and become rather realistic for reaching a more practical end. Now, our mindsets must stress on teamwork, instead of pushing individualism and equality ideals.
6. In general, using genders' unique qualities and differences can enhance the quality of life in society and families a lot.

We cannot change the course of history and the effects of vast social changes. Most likely, we would never benefit from the full potentials of gender differences in our faltering culture, either. However, we might be able to develop at least a more productive perspective regarding gender differences to improve our relationships somewhat. Thus, this book's goal is to offer a basic list of gender qualities and quirks that seem attributable to one gender more readily. This information would be useful for designing better means of teamwork in relationships.

Separating gender qualities from quirks becomes merely a matter of personal taste and opinion, often even subject to our mood swings. Mostly our personal defects and misperceptions make us perceive other people's qualities devilish or see some of their quirks as normal or even useful. Our misperceptions affect our relationships adversely as well, due to the way we judge and react to our partners and their intentions, and in the way we perceive their qualities as quirks or vice versa. Merely our devilish or shallow mentalities contaminate our decision criteria and force us misjudge the real values of our partners and relationships. Therefore, we react improperly (positively or negatively) to our partners' qualities and quirks.

Cultural perceptions of gender qualities, inequalities, and quirks add to the mayhem as well. Many of our newer values are erroneous and misleading without partners' intentions to be so negative and antagonistic. They are merely provoked by those erroneous social mottos. Nevertheless, the outcome of these gender differences in marital relationships is of interest in this book, thus discussed only to help us improve family relationships. As a starting point, in fact, we should initially consider gender attributes mainly as personal qualities, instead of defects or shortcomings that keep ruining our relationships. We just need to reassess our perspective of gender qualities versus quirks and learn how they hinder partners' abilities to relate or communicate.

Therefore, as the general structure of this book, gender qualities are stressed in Part I, then gender quirks are analysed in Part II. Even then, the point for discussing quirks is mostly for grasping the effect of gender differences and the nature of relationship conflicts caused by them, merely for revamping our mentalities and boosting our relationships. Accordingly, Part III's discussions are for increasing couples' awareness and sensitivity in their relationships by learning about the nature of gender quarrels that result mostly from genders' unique quirks and qualities.

As noted in the previous Chapter, men and women are found everywhere on the Personality Chart with large variations in terms of their personality attributes. The proportions of each personality factor used (regardless of the gender) also vary among people quite noticeably. Overall, however, all humans (both genders) use very similar levels of personality factors. Merely the minor differences in the use of the four personality factors (i.e., instincts, logic, model, and ego) account for the rather vast gender differences that cause relationship hurdles.

If we draw the four personality factors suggested in the last chapter on a scale, men and women positions in terms of using personality factors look as shown below:

Humans

Instincts Model | Ego Logic

Women **Men**

This scale shows the percentages of personality factors that men and women use (on the average) in their interactions:

Personality Factors	**Women**	**Men**	**Humans**
Instincts	30%	10%	20%
Model	80%	60%	70%
Ego	70%	90%	80%
Logic	20%	40%	30%

The above ratings reflect humans' natural (instinctual) and acquired urges in general, according to the emerging social conditions, which lead to some unique personality attributes and noticeable gender differences. The scientific origin of these statistics are explained in References on Page 172.

Women are closest to Model and the farthest away from Logic. Conversely, men are closest to Ego and the farthest away from Instincts. That is, while both genders benefit from all personality factors almost equally, men are just a bit more egotistical and logical, compared with women, who are somewhat more social (Model) and intuitive than men. The overall average between the genders provides the rating for Humans—somewhere between the Women and Men points.

Humans' General Qualities

We have all noticed and wondered about gender differences (qualities) like the ones shown in the boxes below. However, it is reiterated that these gender qualities (asserted adjectives) are merely the outcome of some marginal differences between the genders in terms of their use of four personality factors, (i.e., instincts, model, ego, logic). On the other hand, they still cause havoc in relationships, even though they do not reflect gender's absolute personality contrast.

Gender Differences (Qualities)

Women	Men
1. Decisive	1. Pensive
2. Active	2. Passive
3. Neat and organized	3. Loose/Natural
4. Seek independence	4. Seek dependence
5. Idealistic in general	5. Realistic in general
6. Strong identity	6. Poor identity
7. Maternal	7. Creative
8. Seek love	8. Low trust in love
9. High MLove	9. Low MLove
10. Adventurous/Choosy	10. Content

These gender qualities reflect genders' peculiar views of life and social setting as mostly evolved in the new era. Culture and social norms will affect and change them in time. Thus, these gender qualities, as well as their symptoms, are relevant mostly for the present era, e.g., while women are too keen to assert their independence and push for equality. Another key point is that these personality attributes are not only *qualities* that help each gender and every person individually, but also *mechanisms* that become handy if couples learn to combine them to create synergy in their relationships.

People's personality attributes (qualities) manifest in their attitudes and thoughts both positively and negatively, e.g., in the form of originality, spite, jealousy, etc. These reactions or effects of personality attributes are referred to as 'symptoms' in this book and discussed in the next chapter. Studying these widespread symptoms demonstrates the significance of gender differences and their impacts on people's lives and society as a whole. These symptoms are the confusing, complex outcome of gender contacts and frictions. For example, we might be interested to know whether one gender is spiteful more than the other based on the prevalent symptoms of genders' attitude and mentality in the new era.

Nevertheless, the above noted unique gender qualities and their symptoms seem to have major practical implications in daily life, gender interactions, and relationships' health.

List of Women's Qualities

Women's main qualities (personality attributes) affect their ways of thinking, feeling, and behaving somewhat uniquely as discussed in the following:

1. Even the slightly better use of their instincts gives women a higher degree of intuitiveness compared to men.
2. In return, their higher intuitiveness makes women more decisive than men.
3. As an exception, however, women are less decisive than men regarding their careers. On the other hand, they are more adamant to find happiness and a lifestyle akin to their idealistic outlook. Therefore, while less committed to their careers than men, they are more adventurous and choosy about life itself. Naturally, they are more decisive about maternal issues and their children's welfare as well.

4. With higher instinctual tendency and natural handling of Model, women are satiated with all three types of love, i.e., ELove, MLove, and SLove. Furthermore, they can maintain a practical balance among these three types of love better than men can.

   The three types of love are explained in full in other books in these series. Briefly, the following definitions are used in the remainder of this book: (These definitions are posted at the end of the book in References, too, for ease of access when necessary.)

   - SLove (selfless love) is the purest kind of love we feel towards our children, Nature, and possibly our artistic creations. Prefix 'S' could also stand for 'Serving.' With SLove, we Serve (give) love Selflessly with no need or expectation for getting love in return.
   - ELove (egotistic love) reflects our selfish need for love and attention and is mostly a reflection of insecurity. 'E' could also stand for 'Expecting.' With ELove, people demand (Expect) love Egotistically.
   - MLove (model love) is the tactful expressions of love to show compassion and social etiquette. Prefix 'M' could also stand for 'Moderating.' With MLove, people try to Moderate their relationships Modestly accordingly to a tactful Model.
5. Higher instinctual urges have also given women higher emotional tendencies and a higher Model aptitude to adapt and fit better in society.
6. The combination of their higher Model and decisiveness enables and encourages women to be more active in social settings, relationships, and family life. They also like to organize and manage things quickly and move on.
7. Women have traditionally taken less risk as they have felt obliged to take care of their offspring. Nowadays, an inner conflict arises for women who like to be active, take more risks, and be adventurous, but feel their instinctual need to

protect their offspring by averting risks and remaining less active about their careers.

8. Consequently, men and women behave differently outside and inside the house, nowadays. While relatively less competitive and more passive at work, women are quite competitive and active (in charge) at home as part of their inherent nature, but also for balancing their work-related mindset and pressures. Men do the same in the opposite manner. These differences are obviously related to gender differences in terms of social goals and values, too, e.g., women's views of career and family as explained in note # 3 above.
9. Women have a high tendency (bordering obsession) for the cleanliness and tidiness of their households. This dire tendency is most likely the outcome of several personality attributes mixing, including a high desire for likeability and sociability, action orientation, maternal sensibility, and decisiveness.
10. Women seek more independence in order to assert their identity in modern society after many years of inequity, inequality, and oppression by men. However, inherently, they need dependence on a partner at least for emotional support more than ever.
11. Women are more idealistic and optimistic about life and love. They also live longer usually, perhaps because of their positive attitude. (Although the stress from working outside the house and love deprivation would most likely reduce women's life expectancy in the years to come.) Women's positive attitude helps them rebound faster than men after a separation, since they keep hoping for good things and love coming their ways soon.
12. Women have been able to portray a strong identity for themselves. They know what they want and are learning fast how to get it. They are focused and determined. This feels rather natural and easy for them because they must only

focus on their past deprivation, such as independence and equality. Now, all they should do is to find the ways of getting those seemingly precious privileges.

13. Women's maternal instincts and sensitivity are much stronger than men due to genetics, hormones, etc.
14. Besides seeking love more actively due to their instinctual and emotional tendencies, women also seem to have a higher need for things including fashion, household items, and art. Women's search for love and things appear deep and instinctual, as if those needs were totally authentic and heartfelt—often even reaching the level of obsession. This personality attribute is again in line with their higher need for likeability and sociability.
15. The overall effect of the gender differences noted above supports the notion of women being more romantic and needy for a companion in spite of their efforts to appear independent and decisive. At least, they are more open about their search for love than men are. They live in a world of fantasy with many dreams, especially about love and the possibility of finding a prince.
16. As noted above, due to their high Model, women have a higher MLove as well. This means that they express their feelings easier and more masterfully. This ability increases their charm, but also their chances of fulfilling their needs much better. In a way, we can say that women are better equipped to manipulate men.
17. Women are more adventurous, at least mentally, in the sense that they seek variety and pleasures more actively to express themselves and enjoy life. Accordingly, they are choosy in terms of things they like to do and people they befriend, while remain sociable in general very well, too.
18. Women like and seek new challenges due to their active nature, but also for capturing a higher sense of life and happiness.

A great proof of all the above qualities, especially item #2 about women's decisiveness, is evident in the fact that women initiate marital separations in North America in about 70% of the cases. This statistics probably applies to Europe and all other countries where women have the right to ask for divorce. This is the most important life decision in normal conditions, due to so many reasons explained in the author's other books, including *Marriage and Divorce Hardships*. Yet, for women, the decision to ask for separation feels rather easy, necessary, or natural in our current culture.

List of Men's Qualities

Men's main qualities (personality attributes) affect their ways of thinking, feeling, and behaving somewhat uniquely, too, as discussed in the following:

1. Men are slightly more dependent on their logic compared with women who are more intuitive.
2. Even this little difference in the use of logic makes men look different (mostly slow) in terms of decision-making.
3. Accordingly, men are hesitant to draw conclusions and make decisions before they have spent enough time to weigh all the alternatives. Therefore, they appear rather passive.
4. Men are somewhat looser and more natural about daily life routines, including cleanliness and tidiness.
5. Men seek dependence, but need more independence. They have always sought dependence on a partner for sex, companionship, and support in maintaining a household. They are simply too lazy, careless, and incompetent about keeping the household shipshape.
6. Men are more realistic about life and love because they make better use of past information due to their logical

tendencies. They lose hope rather fast in order to reach stability and a state of contentment.

7. At this point, the shock and confusion are keeping men divided, numb, and unorganized about their identity in the new culture. Due to their lower intuition and lower Model, men have been unable to grasp the new culture introduced by women. They have been somewhat caught off-guard and they have not yet been able to devise a new identity for themselves to satisfy women's needs without losing even more of their own identity.
8. Higher logical tendencies of men have led to their higher analytical ability, creativity, and philosophizing during the history of humanity. Within this setting, men have built a higher Ego aptitude and become more arrogant.
9. Their higher Ego and analytical tendency have goaded men to become rather passive, isolated, and to strive for self-actualization.
10. Relative to women, men's need for love and things appear to be moderate and mostly for feeding their Ego (power) and for attracting women, anyway. Of course, men's Ego and greed drive them to acquire more money and power to prove themselves. Like all other males in Nature, men fight, compete, and try to fulfil women's needs, mostly for reaping the rewards of their company and feeding their own Ego.
11. Men's obsessions relate mostly to power, pleasure, and creativity, instead of love and objects per se. Yet, due to their passive attitude about love, and higher deprivation of love, men are inherently more vulnerable emotionally.
12. Men have less faith in love due to their logical orientation, and because they apply the widespread information about relationship failures more analytically. In older cultures, love had much less value for men, and that mentality has been passed on to men in the new generations largely as well. They have always been less romantic, anyway, thus

the effect of the new culture and the movies about love and romance has been lesser on men than it has been on women.

13. Yet, men are equally sensitive and very much emotional, if not more than women are in many instances. Meanwhile, their lack of trust in love and their inabilities, or lower chances, to express their emotions reduce men's ability to relate to their partners, which then leads to stress and deep inner conflicts for them, too.
14. Men's high Ego, and low Model, curtails their ability to seek love as openly as they need. They are more practical and realize soon that finding a princess is merely a myth. Nevertheless, as noted above, they are more vulnerable emotionally.
15. In all, men seem pensive and preoccupied with immediate issues and certain primary features of life, compared to women who desire to be involved with more activities and new adventures.
16. Accordingly, men are more content (than women) with the status quo and the way things are, rather than doing new stuff, including travelling and tourism, just for the heck of it in hopes of more happiness.

Note: While the above 18 and 16 qualities enumerated for women and men relate more directly to that particular group, they also reflect on the opposite gender's personality attribute indirectly, by default. For example, saying women are more decisive implies that men are more doubtful and slower in making their decisions compared to women, and vice versa. In other word, women's seemingly hasty, emotional, or intuitive attitude about decision-making makes men appear odd in this respect! The opposite is naturally true as well! Women appear weird as well, i.e., looking too impatient and pushy to get things done.

The statistic noted at the end of the last section about women's tendency (in 70% of cases) to request for separation confirms the points made above about men's qualities as well, especially their passivity and indecisiveness regarding the quality and purpose of their relationships.

CHAPTER THREE
Personality Symptoms

All those unique and useful personality attributes for men and women listed in the previous chapter make them think, feel, and behave in creative and emotional ways. They become who they are in the form they present themselves to others, but also in terms of reacting to other people's attitude, especially in their family relationships. Their life experiences, personal qualities, and inner conflicts make their thoughts and attitudes appear bizarre to others, however. Thus, many of our personal qualities turn into, or are perceived as, quirks.

Accordingly, pressure mounts in relationships as partners are annoyed by each other's quirks, instead of appreciating each other's qualities. Even worse, couples do not know how to combine their qualities in order to relate and work together in a teamwork environment. Thus, the symptoms of gender differences manifest in destructive forms. All those personal qualities, in fact, begin to clash and relationship conflicts grow at many levels. Using the men's and women's lists of qualities (and differences) in the last chapter, we can see how those qualities are suddenly envisioned and treated as idiosyncrasies. The list of *symptoms* related to each of the qualities listed for men and women, as depicted in the following pages, show how every one of those personality attributes (qualities) turns into a source of conflict and havoc in relationships.

By the way, the 'Qualities' and 'Symptoms' for women and men listed in the following pages should be viewed as general tendencies and not scientific notions. It is impossible to generalize easily in social sciences, especially about human behaviour and personality. The list of gender tendencies and differences noted here are by no means complete, either. They are only examples of the most common observations about genders' interactions and communications. Along with this disclaimer, the assertions in this book are still in line with the author's and other scholars' experiments and observations. They are presented in the same order of the ten qualities listed below. Yet, some points may be repeated when they apply to more than one item on the list. All the discussions in this book about gender differences are based on this chapter's general assumptions and conclusions.

Women's Personality

Women's distinct qualities stir the following symptoms:

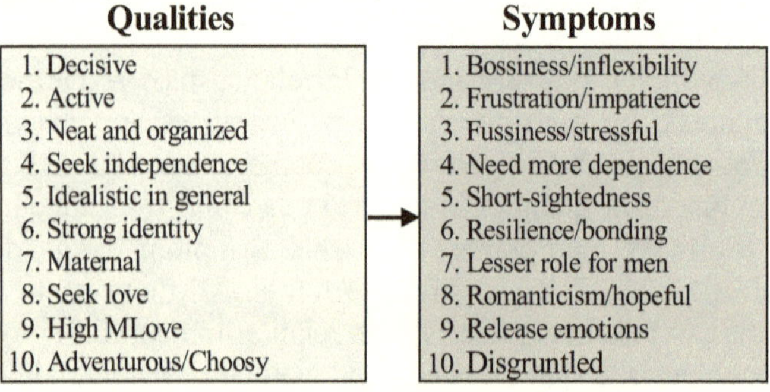

Qualities	Symptoms
1. Decisive	1. Bossiness/inflexibility
2. Active	2. Frustration/impatience
3. Neat and organized	3. Fussiness/stressful
4. Seek independence	4. Need more dependence
5. Idealistic in general	5. Short-sightedness
6. Strong identity	6. Resilience/bonding
7. Maternal	7. Lesser role for men
8. Seek love	8. Romanticism/hopeful
9. High MLove	9. Release emotions
10. Adventurous/Choosy	10. Disgruntled

1. The effect of women's decisiveness is that they look bossy and inflexible. Their intuitiveness makes them more certain about their conclusions, thus become more opinionated. They are bossy and rigid also because they are frustrated with their procrastinating husbands. Often, however, men perceive women's inflexibility as a sign of insensitivity.

Surely, this perceived low sensitivity is not contradictory to the fact that women are usually better in expressing their emotions with their higher Model and MLove when they feel necessary.

In fact, women's occasional show or appearance of insensitivity may come as a surprise and contradictory to their show of oversensitivity discussed in the following item (# 2). Yet, these seemingly personality contradictions are also the realities that make women too complex and mysterious.

2. Higher instinctual urges and keener perceptions of life have made women sensitive and often oversensitive to the point of overreacting to simplest inconvenience and low attention. Women's oversensitivity raises their frustration and inner conflicts when men are becoming preoccupied and less sensitive in general.
3. Besides low impatience, women's (over)active mindset and personality fluster them when their plans and wishes do not proceed as fast or agreeable to them as they dream. Thus, their fanciful, dynamic mindset is an added factor in making women bossy, sensitive, and even more impatient.
4. Women's craze for cleanliness and tidiness makes them come across as uptight and fussy. Their tendency to rely so much on their intuitions also aggravates their edginess.
5. Women's struggles to gain, and show, their independence jeopardize their innate need for dependence. Independence is obviously synonymous with self-reliance. So, the more women play the role of independent partners, the more men find themselves alienated in terms of helping women with their dependency need. Many reasons exist for this debilitating condition. The main reason is that, as civilized people, we try to help or interfere in someone's affairs only when he/she asks for help. It feels awkward to interfere with the affairs of a spouse who keeps insisting on being self-reliant at so many levels all the time. Sadly, partners

are getting confused about 'when' to offer or seek help, especially emotional support. Their rising misperceptions and misinterpretations about help sought or offered make couples both too anxious and oversensitive regarding their relationships. The bottomline is that the women's need for dependence on a reliable partner has been left unfulfilled. All along, their higher Model and emotional tendencies also reinforce their need for dependence even more. The dilemma of dependence versus independence is discussed in more details in Chapter Seven due to its importance.

6. Neither gender has yet decided regarding a right balance for their dependence/independence needs in order to keep their inner conflicts at minimum. In particular, they must balance their gender-oriented needs in order to maximize their communication efficiency and relate easier. At the same time, it is questionable whether the natural properties of genders would ever let them reach a practical balance for their dependence and independence needs at the levels that are also acceptable to the other gender. This particular symptom of gender needs, nowadays, has big implications for many other aspects of relationships, mainly because couples' reactions towards this imbalance are too harsh, hostile, and futile. As long as this imbalance prevails in people's personal lives, the matter would cause only more alienation and havoc in relationships, especially in terms of relating to one another.
7. Women's idealism and higher optimism in life make them less concerned about the potential risks ahead. They often focus on the near future, perhaps now. For example, they seem to show an obsession to own a house regardless of the potential financial burdens. Their short-sightedness is a symptom of their over-optimism, which surely makes planning and risk management difficult in relationships.
8. Women's struggles and success in recent decades to define a proper identity for themselves have led to their higher

resilience and bonding among them. They have proven capable of supporting one another and bonding for their common objectives. They have built many new techniques and games to achieve what they want and stay vigilant about the progress of their plans. They have learned to be independent and make money, and they are somewhat more optimistic about life, too. To protect their plans, they have also become calculating and assertive—or often even aggressive. As a whole, women have developed a specific, concrete identity (or at least an image of it) for themselves and are bonding together to make sure it is promoted and protected. Women's cohesion and lower Ego have been helping them in reinforcing their new identity.

9. The stronger identity for women at the cost of men losing theirs would continue to damage relationships and both genders would suffer from this imbalance. Meanwhile, neither gender would find its identity, because in the final analyses they need each other to create their real identities.
10. Ironically, and most importantly, men and women would succeed in building their relationships only if they develop proper (unselfish) gender identities in the first place.
11. A basic question is if the genders must (would) eventually develop complementary (or compromising) identities and attitudes in order to relate better. *In a century or so maybe!*
12. The result of women pushing their rather radical identity and men losing theirs might be interesting. We may predict that men's Ego would be curbed eventually, thus a simpler relationship atmosphere might emerge. It is a possibility. Yet, the change, if any, would not be felt in this century for many reasons. First, Ego is an innate trait in men built during a long history of humanity. So it cannot be curbed easily despite the women's attempt to tame men. It would take many decades to tone down men's egoism, if at all possible. Second, men's Ego would not allow the existing situation, i.e., their loss of identity, continue for too long.

Even the existing passive reactions by men may soon lead to the emergence of new relationship approaches. Men are equally intelligent and maybe even capable of colluding, eventually, in order to reclaim some kind of identity for themselves. Anyhow, both genders would realize the need for creating practical balances and attitudes. Men's loss of identity is, thus, a temporary situation. A new identity for men would emerge within a century or so. Would it be passive and submissive somewhat, largely, or at all?! Can they show their aptitude to grow a *progressive* identity to counter that of women's somehow? It is quite possible!

13. A similar comment can be made about women's present Model tendency. In their new approach, they already look (or pretend to be) equally Ego*tistical*, which indicates that many of their new personality traits might lose steam and erode naturally gradually. Then again, women's instinctual tendencies are too deep to be drastically subdued by their attempt to create a mannish identity for themselves. They would always be the tender mother that nature has meant them to be, despite the growing perceived image of their insensitivity on many occasions. Nonetheless, the existing state of transition will come to a practical equilibrium eventually. In that steady state, both genders have clear identities that stir a higher synergy in their relationships.
14. Women's powerful maternal urge pushes them in terms of not only luring men for the ultimate goal of procreation, but also finding a lesser value in men afterward. Nature is possibly making women so demanding and commanding to run the whole family efficiently. Thus, they treat men like another child. They keep nagging and pushing them away into an emotional standby, at least temporarily. To women, babies are their ultimate creations that fulfil their need for self-actualization and dependence largely. Thus, children get their utmost attention. Despite women's strong need for dependency on men (mostly for socializing and

ELove), this urge is somewhat dampened, at least while their children keep them busy and while they know that their faithful husbands are still around at a safe distance.

15. Women's natural (historical) urge to treat men like another child might have contributed to men's seclusion a lot. They became more self-reliant and developed a higher need for self-actualization, creativity, and Ego. They have also felt more need for emotional and financial self-reliance.
16. Conversely, women developed more Model orientation to support one another and their offspring with lesser need for stray males. Then again, men's view of (and frustration about) women's moodiness and insensitivity might have made men more reclusive and aggressive towards women.
17. Women's belief and obsession to find love make them too romantic and hopeful at the cost of losing their chance of getting a realistic perspective of relationships, nowadays. They overestimate men's ability to handle this new, rather fanciful expectation about the importance of love.
18. As noted before, women goad one another to be assertive and leave their husbands fast if they cannot (or refuse to) respond to their desires. The question is women's motives. Do they provoke each other out of kindness, jealousy, malice, rivalry, ignorance, or a mix of these incentives? A cynical viewpoint is that they often do it to screw up one another intentionally for personal reasons or to promote women's presumed new identity. The jury is out on this one. Yet, some good explanations might exist for doing it for their own benefits and not necessarily out of kindness, though these analyses are beyond the scope of this book! Yet, women believe that pushing a low-tolerance attitude would enforce their identity and feminism and keep their spouses under control. This mentality might backfire and reduce the chances of harmony in relationships even more.
19. Women have a higher tendency for jealousy and rivalry, in spite of their high aptitude for bonding. Especially, they are

competitive amongst themselves in terms of objects and passion they seek from men. They also compete amongst themselves for pushing their identity. They try to show off their individuality and dominance in their relationships in order to excel other women on these factors. These crude games infect their relationships, though.

20. The human hormones and their cyclical changes affect genders' brain activities differently. Especially women are more susceptible to depression, anxiety, and mood swings because of hormonal changes during maternity, menstrual cycle, and menopause.
21. The genders' distinct 'brain functions' make them react to various life conditions and stress quite differently as well. As an example, the cortisol level, which measures stress intensity, is typically two times higher in women than it is in men. This is due to the way women perceive pain much deeper and the way they go about calming themselves.
22. While men try to face their stress by solving their sources or ignoring them, women need to discuss their problems. This chance to talk releases serotonin in their brains that calms their limbic system. Still, twice as many women are on antidepressants compared with men based on statistics.
23. In all, hormones usually make women more decisive and optimistic about life, so they set high expectations for their relationships, too. Along with new slogans and approaches in society, women are more idealistic and seek love and happiness more obsessively, nowadays, too, which leads to their higher depression and uptightness. Hormones have also raised women's ability to bond and be outgoing.
24. Women now endure lots more inner conflicts than men do, since their new identity and social role do not coincide with their instinctual, maternal, and romantic tendencies. They also have a tougher time (and more inner conflicts) for aligning their needs for dependence and independence. The symptoms of women's high inner conflicts appear in

their higher stress and frustration, which naturally lead to many types of relationship conflicts, too.

All the above symptoms clash regularly with the symptoms of men's personality attributes (qualities), as discussed in the next section, and together they cause havoc in relationships. Both genders try to adjust themselves and their lifestyles with these irritating symptoms *as if facing an inevitable reality of life!* Still, we might be able to use these clashing symptoms to our advantage if we use our intelligence better more humbly.

Men's Personality

Men's distinct qualities stir the following symptoms:

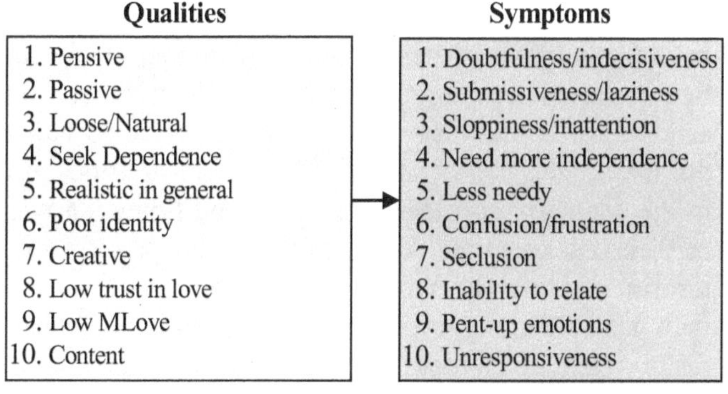

1. Men's contemplation and caution for making decisions portray them as indecisive and lacking spontaneity.
2. Of course, men are trying to be practical by disallowing spontaneity affect their decisions and cause tragedy. Some men actually realize their partial responsibility for their wives' anxiety (due to men's relative indecisiveness), thus try to make up for it by passivity and adaptation (including even submission). That is, to offset their indecisiveness, they learn to absorb and tolerate their partners' reactions, including women's relative bossiness. Therefore, the level of men's submissiveness has been rising in recent decades.

3. Unlike women who are intuitively decisive, men are often forced to decide due to timelines, obligations, desperation, etc. Their attitude also manifests in their procrastination for choosing and proposing to a woman. Women make their decisions about the suitability of a man rather quickly.
4. Men's tendencies towards logic, analysis, and creativity make them feel and look rather self-absorbed or careless.
5. Men's excess Ego over Model ultimately turns men more inwardly and passive, too, with a tougher job to adapt to martial life, and thus instigating more family clashes.
6. Men's passivity portrays them as lazy and submissive. Their passivity is then reinforced and proven when they readily let their wives run the family affairs, mostly because they (men) are actually lazy, even for arguments.
7. Although men are less intuitive in general, they look more natural and looser in their attitude and are more inclined to live in the wilderness, rather inhibited. Accordingly, they acquire a different taste and priority for life than women do. Especially, the symptoms of their life priorities erupt in the way they consider cleanliness and tidiness a waste of their precious time. Yet, they can easily waste a lot of time on odd hobbies, such as watching sports and drinking with pals. All along, men's seemingly misplaced priorities make women even more puzzled and perturbed.
8. The effect of men's loose, easygoing attitude is that they also come across as too insensitive and sloppy regarding issues that their wives are so sensitive about, especially in terms of household appearance and cleanliness.
9. Men's search for dependence on a companion is mostly a symptom of their high need for independence and freedom. They wish to rely on their wives to manage the mundane family affairs, so that they (men) can attend to immediate affairs outside the house. Yet, their need for dependence is less fulfilled, nowadays, as women insist on independence, too, which reduces the supply of reliable, consistent source

of support for men. Men have a hard time fulfilling this goal. Thus, they seek dependence even more desperately—almost at the same level women seek more independence.

Yet, men, by nature and their higher Ego, need more independence psychologically. They like to be left alone to spend time on their own contemplations, creating, and feeding their Ego. In all, men seek dependence (on a mate) mainly for getting the opportunity of fulfilling their need for independence. In older times, men got the dependence they sought rather easily. Thus, they could fulfil their need for independence easier, too. However, they have now lost the opportunity of satisfying both their independence and dependence needs. Nowadays, they must pay a high price to get the dependence they seek in a companion. The price is paid in the form of giving up more of the independence they crave instinctually and had enjoyed easily in the past. The level of independence they must forgo to get a relative dependence often seems out of proportion to them, thus they are getting quite confused, while losing a big chunk of their identities, too. Meanwhile, couples' struggles with their confusing gender identities have also raised havoc in relationships, as explained in the following pages.

Two interesting questions the above points raise, then, are, 'Why men and women have difficulty relating to one another when their natural needs are complementary so nicely, indeed?', and, 'Since both women and men *need* more dependence than they presently get, why cannot they stress on fulfilling their dependence needs, while discuss their independence needs more civilly, too?' The answer is that both genders want both dependence and independence simultaneously rather excessively and erratically. Although they both *need* dependence and independence at specific instants, they *seeks* one of them more prominently rather randomly. Their needs (for dependence and independence) are rather opposite to what they *seek* innately and express openly. They just hide their natural needs from each other. So oddly, these days both genders *need* more dependence, but just cannot fulfil each other's exact needs. Weirder, nowadays, both genders need more independence, too, yet do not know how to achieve them together. They cannot align their needs for dependence and independence, since they have no proper identities and means of relating civilly —*and vice versa*. The independence/dependence dilemma is discussed further in Chapter 7 due to its importance.

10. Since both genders have difficulty aligning their needs for dependence and independence in their relationships, they can neither satisfy their personal goals, nor create the right kind of atmosphere for teamwork and synergy.
11. The effect of men's higher tendency to stay realistic about life's promises vs. traps, along with their general cynicism, goads them to focus on relative stability and contentment, often by submissiveness around family—just to save their energies to fight outside the house on more urgent issues.
12. Contrary to women, who have succeeded in defining a kind of identity for themselves, men's inability to build an identity has confused and frustrated them. Men's higher Ego prevents them from organizing their thoughts and finding common grounds. They are passive and lazy about this matter, too, of course. They have so far not taken women's drive for a new identity seriously enough, either. They naively imagined that the situation was somewhat under control. Now, however, they must forgo a lot of their independence to acquire the dependence they seek in a companion. They do not know how to develop a new identity to cope with the emerging environment. Instead, they are becoming more submissive and passive. Thus, the effect of this situation is that men are becoming further isolated and frustrated with their relationships. Women are also frustrated about this situation for different reasons, but mainly about men's passivity.

13. Men's lower sense of maternity and limited involvement with child rearing would continue to keep their role in the family secondary to women's at best.
14. Men's lower sensitivity, due to their slightly higher logical tendency, realism, and mistrust in love, has led to their general scepticism about love, thus a lower level of MLove and capacity to relate in relationships.
15. The effect of men's self-absorption and low Model curtails their abilities to show love openly. Thus, their emotions dampen, while they remain emotionally more vulnerable than women who can express MLove more proactively.
16. Men's lower Model and Mlove, plus pent-up emotions, raise their frustration and aggression, especially when they strive to be logical at the time their wives are seeking lots more support and affection even though they are bossy and insensitive themselves frequently.
17. Accordingly, men end up being preoccupied, passive, and content due to their senses of obligation, desperation, and Egos. Thus, they are, or appear, rather unresponsive to the high demands of their wives for more attention.
18. In line with note # 24 (page 34) about women's growing inner conflicts (due to their evolving, controversial new identity), men's inner conflicts are rising, too, due to their loss of identity and the ambiguity of their roles in family. However, the symptoms of their inner conflict are more moderate and concealed due to their passivity, pragmatism, and confusion.

The above rudimentary observations about gender differences have been made based on the list of gender qualities and symptoms suggested in this chapter, as well as the author's grasp of studies about human hormones. These observations also signify and verify the emergence of a peculiar trend in relationships, mostly in terms of our new approach towards sexuality and its potential outcome. In addition, they reflect women's higher optimism about life and the possibility of finding real love regardless of their age and their past negative experiences. Their idealism goads them to live in their fantasy world and keep looking for romance and beautiful things. In addition, they are very active, nowadays, in encouraging one another to seek perfection, independence, individuality, and love. They encourage and support one another to leave their relationships when they cannot give them all the things and compassion they believe they deserve. They naively assume, all along, that men are psychologically capable of delivering all those things and compassion. Therefore, when they do not, women attribute it to men's spite, passivity, insensitivity, and stupidity.

On the other hand, men are more practical and give up on the idea of finding the perfect mate. Thus, they try to be a little more tolerant and accept mediocre relationships longer. Their minds are preoccupied with immediate responsibilities or silly hobbies like sports. Their Ego and passivity, of course, cause relationship conflicts. However, the bottomline is that men cannot change themselves too much, not enough for the liking of women. Accordingly, couples face undue conflicts and separations. Women, in particular, keep saying that life is too short and you live only once. Therefore, they keep chasing their fantasy about finding men who can fulfil their dreams. They do not take notice that, while wasting their lives in search of acceptable men (if not ideal ones), they might be depriving themselves and their kids from the simple privileges of companionship and accomplishing some basic objectives that two people can attain better together if only they stopped arguing too much about irresolvable gender differences and relationship issues. Thus, more loneliness and depression are emerging in society, while women keep searching for their imaginary mates, and men are becoming more sceptical about getting into relationships.

PART II

Gender Quirks

CHAPTER FOUR
Humans' General Quirks

Humans have a large variety of quirks that make them unique, interesting, impure, and evil too often. Many variables, including genetics and rearing, develop human idiosyncrasies. In particular, social teachings and values influence our ways of thinking, feeling, and behaving. Then, our efforts to build our families scramble our emotions even further and cause havoc in our relationships. Thus, the rising frictions and disharmony in modern relationships.

The main goal in Part II is to develop an outline of general obstacles that gender differences impose on relationships. We like to know how the symptoms of gender qualities actually turn into real or perceived quirks that hinder couples' abilities to relate. Some of these *rather general* quirks are reviewed in this chapter, while each gender's specific quirks are reviewed in the next two chapters. The existing social setting and values discussed in this chapter are both the cause and the symptom of the emerging gender differences, after all.

We cannot dismiss the simple fact that men and women perceive the world, set their life priorities, and make decisions differently. These differences have widened in modern society where self-worth, equality, and independence find high value. In addition, humans' high Ego and low ability for compromise fuel gender differences and pose major obstacles for a smooth process of communication and teamwork needed urgently in new relationships. This mayhem will persist until couples' mindsets are probably aligned with relationships' unique needs within the next few decades—by some miracle maybe.

The present social setting is highly conducive to expansion of gender differences, which would in turn stir more marital conflicts, personal agonies, and social mayhem. Breaking this vicious cycle for a chance to grasp the roots of marital issues, including the symptoms of gender differences, require sensible socioeconomic systems, which sound like an ambitious dream to entertain about the greedy, arrogant humans in the modern world.

The bottomline is that, for improving marital and societal health, couples must at least realize how sickly current culture and ideologies are abusing gender differences and increasing conflicts in relationships. Grasping and acknowledging at least the following facts about human nature and the effects of our alleged civilization on our behaviour is essential for increasing couples' compassion by higher knowledge of marital hurdle, while hoping to salvage humans' gloomy fate as well:

1. Humans' four personality factors (instincts, model, ego, and logic) build and reflect their unique qualities and quirks.
2. Although gender differences regarding these factors are not substantial, even those minor differences lead to noticeable variations in gender's attitude, feeling, and thinking.
3. Each gender has a rather uniform mindset for interpreting the world and setting its life priorities based on the culture and prevalent social values.
4. Accordingly, each gender has some common *qualities* that make that group appear rather eccentric to the other gender.
5. The *symptoms* of genders' unique qualities, such as men's lower intuitiveness or women's higher decisiveness in the new era might be viewed as quirks according to cultural norms and people.

6. A set of inner (psychological) and outer (socioeconomic) forces drives everybody to perceive the world and others uniquely. Thus, we often feel, think, and act in certain ways that others might find abnormal or offensive. This basic awareness might increase both our tolerance and sympathy toward our partners, while we gauge our own likely quirks.
7. Accordingly, gender differences affect people's motives behind their actions and feelings, too. For example, while both genders have equal sexual drives, they usually have different motives for acting upon it. All these varied gender motives are behind the harmful gender symptoms, e.g., men's higher tendency for aggression or laziness, as noted in Chapter Three.
8. Women's natural superiority in creating and safeguarding their offspring appears to contribute to the fact that men lose their priority in relationships when children are born. This reality leads to a variety of misperceptions, deep inner conflicts, and frequent frictions in relationships.
9. An outer force that affects relationships adversely without anyone's fault is that women are in a state of transition in terms of the progressive role they wish to play in society and relationships.
10. Women's new role in relationships is not understood even by the majority of women, let alone by men who are now expected to not only know what the new format should be, but also respond positively.
11. It would be an inherently difficult task, for men especially, to achieve the changes required in terms of gender roles, even in a timelier manner, even if they agreed to the changes women are asking of them.
12. Therefore, couples adhere to all kinds of destructive games, including manipulation, intimidation, and retaliation in hopes of managing, controlling, and enduring their gloomy relationships.

13. Couples want to set the tone of their relationships through power struggles, with the ultimate intention of dominating their relationships and partners.
14. Within this confusing situation, all kinds of aggressions by both genders are convoluting the transition process. Instead of progress, we witness more sabotages and retaliation, games, divorces, and family murder suicides.
15. The bottomline is that men have now lost their identity (whatever it was, good or bad) and do not understand the sensibility of what is expected of them. And women are also frustrated, since they cannot prove and enforce a new identity, which they naively *believe* they know what it is.
16. The result of the current confusion (about gender identities) is that partners finally get fed up with their struggles to convince each other logically. Therefore, they try to either dominate each other or resort to divorce.
17. It appears that, nowadays, too many people are always struggling to either find a companion or get rid of him/her.
18. Therefore, all our lives, we look for an imaginary idol to accept as our companion, or we try to rebuild (change) our partners to fit that image. Especially, a new trend is to make men softer, so that they can respond to women's desires and perceptions of relationships better.
19. A special situation seems to have emerged: Due to men's passivity, women find it necessary to become aggressive in order to attain the assertiveness they need urgently.
20. Men and women are inherently incompatible in terms of nature. Therefore, partners' effort to find their compatible companion is mostly a shot in the dark, anyway. And still the new relationship approaches and games make the job of finding our soul mate even tougher.
21. Peculiar messages that men and women exchange by their attitudes and games are putting further distance between them. These role-playings and games are too difficult to understand or respond to.

22. The main reason and need for these games is that couples do not grasp the roots of relationship conflicts and gender differences, and they do not know how to face the natural symptoms of genders' personality attributes.
23. The games couples play to maintain the balance of power is an ongoing, exhausting process. Partners simply seem incapable of putting down their guards, to live and relate naturally by satisfying the relationships' unique needs in the new era.
24. Another problem is that even when a partner plans to stop playing games and behave naturally, he/she cannot deal with his/her partner who is addicted to relationship games.
25. The irony is that people always notice and criticize other people's games and phoniness, but not their own. Usually, they are aware of the games and roles they are playing, but naively assume that they can get away with them. They trust their playacting too much. Even worse, they believe people are too simple or busy to see through them.
26. Ironically, people usually play their idiotic roles and games in hopes of raising their relationships' chances for success. Yet, by doing so, they actually raise the chances of being discredited and rejected.
27. A frustrating situation in relationships develops when a partner insists on playing a role or game and his/her partner does not fall for it.
28. Relationships fail because too many of partners' games clash. The more games they play to cope with social and family issues, the more conflicts arise, which then lead to even more games.
29. Usually one partner starts a game with a special intention —mostly for handling the symptoms of his/her partner's personality attributes. Then, the other partner starts his/her own game instead of playing along. Accordingly, partners are astonished that their games are detected and resisted.

Therefore, they keep introducing more games until they are exhausted and angry.

30. People consider their acts of charming and manipulating others their absolute right and an effective tool, while they believe they are good at it, too. So, when they fail, they just get too angry and nasty about it. All that charm suddenly turns into hostility and ruins even their basic capacity and interest for relating.
31. The way people snub each other as a way of relating—to set the tone of their friendships and marriages—is funny.
32. Instead of expecting happiness from relationships, couples must realize that they should actually be willing to pay a big price for it. This is a major requirement and personal sacrifice they should be ready to accept before entering a relationship. Always a high price must be paid for the few fringe benefits of relationships.
33. People are ignoring the simple fact that retaliations cannot help them solve their relationship or personal problems.
34. It is quite silly when someone retaliates in order to draw his/her partner's attention and force compassion or passion in their marriage. Actually, anyone capable of retaliating harshly is inherently empty of compassion.
35. Love and spite (anger) are incompatible, and whoever uses anger to force (or keep) love is simply incapable of giving or taking love.
36. With the advent of various dating facilities, people meet and learn about many candidates for dating. While this flexibility seems helpful to find a match, it also increases people's false hopes about their chances to find a qualified person soon. Therefore, they become too fussy and keep joggling a bunch of relationships. Meanwhile, people who are truly suitable for being in relationships are becoming scarcer, too.
37. People keep multiple romantic relationships since they are doubtful about the viability of any of them. In addition, it

feels more efficient to appraise a few seemingly qualified candidates simultaneously, as it usually takes many years to get to know someone, if at all.

38. Keeping multiple affairs might also help a person rebound faster if one of his/her favourite relationships fails. He/she has other mates to lean on awhile at least. All these excuses sound reasonable, but what a weird world we have created.
39. Our hope to eventually find a soul mate is a naive incentive that prevents us from making genuine commitments and efforts in a relationship or keeping our promises.
40. Under these tough conditions, perhaps the best definition for a soul mate is, 'Someone we can rather get along with and trust a little, finally!'
41. Another cause of the increasing mistrust in relationships and society is that people recognize the games everybody plays, including multiple dating. Therefore, it is hard for people to take their relationships seriously. Oddly enough, however, everybody is also too eager and hopeful to find a reliable companion, as if s/he would arrive from another planet. People's struggle and optimism to find love, trust, and happiness are both admirable and depressing. It is sad because people seem to miss, or eager to ignore, the new realities of relationships.
42. Many people, especially women, perceive the flattery they receive a sign of their chances to find a better mate once they leave their present partners. Then after separation, they realize how they have been misled, mostly by their own idiotic misperceptions and optimism.
43. People, especially some luckier, shallow men, are enjoying the present situation with multiple dating and all. However, both genders (mostly women) are also getting anxious about their failures to find qualified partners, while women are facing men's increasing passivity, too.
44. People's reaction to the present relationship conditions is just to do more of the same things, i.e., more games, more

multiple dating, more lying and mistrust, and more shallow relationships. Thus, the rising level of frustration in society.

45. The complexity of the relationship environment and our passivity about it are the main reasons it will take at least a century to find real solutions for relationships.
46. Many humble individuals are out there who could be in good relationships together if they were not deterred by their (often-justified) paranoia about the ominous state of relationships and their lack of trust in people.
47. People do not know how to be tactful or observe even basic etiquettes, but keep insisting on the purity of their soul and love expressions.
48. While everybody is obsessed about finding his/her soul mate, the chance of it ever happening is slim. However, we all have difficulty accepting this fact, since we want to stay positive. Our romantic search for a soul mate is preventing us from perceiving relationships realistically and facing life as an independent person.
49. Couples' promises or commitments are not reliable these days. Especially, taking the phrase ‘I love you’ seriously, as a sign of commitment, is naïve.
50. People do not change unless they feel the need for it through years of meditation and self-awareness. Therefore, partners' retaliations and intimidations to change each other are just a reflection of their own naivety.
51. Nowadays, people, especially women, are too idealistic, ambitious, neurotic, depressed, and stressed due to their new lifestyles and fantasies.
52. Women make a big fuss about their need for independence, but also demand to be spoiled. Ironically, they do not see the conflict, either.
53. People are getting more insecure due to our tainted culture; therefore, they have become needier for love and attention. When they often cannot fulfil all their dreams at the desired level, they feel even more lost and frustrated.

54. Relationships have become too important, nowadays, since people's basic needs are satisfied in modern societies rather easily. Without too many pressing issues and hardships to give them a real perspective of life, they fuss too much about love and happiness.
55. Relationships appear like the best antidote for loneliness, too, because we cannot live independently anymore despite all our pretensions.
56. However, providing constant attention to our insecure partners is also a major responsibility that causes anxiety besides all the extra work.
57. Relationships also force lifestyle changes and adaptation, often for fitting with our partners' (and their family's) habits and conflicting preferences.
58. Couples' insecurities and needs for retaliation have reached such extremes that they kidnap, terrorize, or harm their own children just for intimidating their estranged partners. The intensity of child custody battles also demonstrates how ineffective our marital mechanisms are.
59. The above points reveal the huge challenge we, especially the new generations, must face in order to find better ways of relating, instead of retaliating, in their relationships.
60. For facing all these new challenges, it is necessary to view gender differences in a more productive perspective, rather than being cynical and critical too much about them. We should view these differences as a potent innate force that can help genders complement each other and increase their relationships' efficiency. Yet, the big challenge is to make both genders really feel the need to revamp their present destructive mentalities and exploit their difference to their advantage.

The above facts reflect our legitimate concerns about the way our deteriorating social setting is widening gender differences and conflicts. Couples feel the rising turmoil and try to deal with them somehow, but mostly blame their partners for their relationship conundrums. Their feelings and complaints are natural and understandable, but futile. We hurt one another in relationships due to our dogged reluctance to see the bigger picture and realize that relationship conflicts are, nowadays, the symptoms of partners' idealism and wildly progressive mentalities. We are merely criticizing one another for who we are and insist on changing one another to our liking. We do not wish to accept that people have the right to be and live as they wish, especially since their odd attitudes, feelings, and actions are driven by some deep personality attributes that they cannot readily change. The problem is that our qualities and quirks clash, especially in marriages where partners are too close physically and mentally and wish to relate properly. The problem is that everybody ignores, or actually often loves, his/her own idiosyncrasies, but resent other people's—even their similar quirks, such as pomposity that is becoming a fatal social pandemic.

Ironically, even natural human qualities often emerge as personal quirks, especially in families when couples struggle to build their relationships and fulfil their needs and duties through endless interactions. These varied quirks are either real or the product of our perceptions due to our hasty, biased, and selfish judgments. Thus, another task for married people is to become more patient and think somewhat less selfishly to establish if their partner's growing quirks are real or only their own perceptions due to unrealistic expectations from their partners or relationships in general. Nevertheless, neither our relationships, nor our partners can ever be flawless, let alone perfect, especially these days with so much complexities we have imposed upon relationships. Only learning about gender quirks and raising our sensitivities about them can somewhat alleviate the pressures on relationships.

Nevertheless, our harsh reactions to the gloomy reality of relationships in the new era would not solve anything. Instead, we must adjust our mentalities a bit to envision the potential benefits of gender differences and use them to raise synergy in relationships. We must remember that personal attributes and quirks, like Ego, are often personal qualities that everybody needs for managing his/her life the best s/he can based on his/her limited intelligence in such a corrupt society. For example, both women's decisiveness and men's passivity are valuable attributes for them if they are applied properly in a timely manner. They are complementary assets that can lead to better decisions at the end. However, we often see them as gender quirks when women's decisiveness often clashes with men's passivity.

Of course, each gender must also recognize the symptoms of their unique personality attributes and the way they cause frictions in relationships. They must recognize the impressions that their quirks, e.g., bossiness or procrastination, make on their partners and cause deep conflicts. Partners should admit that many of their seemingly logical habits may be symptoms of their personality defects and quirks that can damage their relationships if they ignore them, or just consider them natural or personal choices for living. As soon as we decide to be in a relationship, we lose lots of our natural rights and freedom for doing many things the way we like. Instead, lots of diplomacy, tactfulness, and teamwork is required just to curb the irritating symptoms of our own natural personality traits and tolerate the symptoms of our partners' natural personality attributes. Lots of give and take are necessary to balance the symptoms of gender differences and other causes of relationship conflicts.

In particular, courting partners must be acquainted with the prevalent gender quirks and qualities that infect relationships in advance and take them very seriously. They must anticipate and prepare for all the expected havoc beforehand. Then, they should test their patience for dealing with those rather idiotic, but common, symptoms in new relationships before getting married. They should understand and sympathize with their spouses' idiosyncrasies and remember how some symptoms, e.g., decisiveness or procrastination, could lead to all sorts of misperceptions and hasty judgments in relationships without partners' intentions to hurt each other. Many examples of these conditions have been discussed in this book.

Overall, the main purpose of reviewing gender qualities and their symptoms, which ultimately lead to some seeming quirks, is to raise couples' awareness, patience, and sympathy for handling their relationship conundrums somewhat easier with proper mindsets. If both sides (genders) see these fine points a bit more compassionately and show more flexibility and patience, the level of stress and conflicts would subside dramatically in relationships.

Chapter Ten provides another 160 facts regarding human quirks and gender disparities causing so much relationship conflicts and social stress. The next two chapters will discuss some of the genders' real and perceived quirks.

CHAPTER FIVE
Womanly Quirks

Gender qualities and symptoms discussed in Chapters Two and Three often clash when people communicate and try to protect their rights and interests. The symptoms of people's qualities (personality attributes) often turn into major personal quirks and shake the foundation of their relationships. Thus, more details about these gender oriented symptoms and quirks are presented in this and the following chapter.

It should be emphasized again, however, that the personal quirks discussed in this book are merely common tendencies that erupt variably in both genders from time to time. On the other hand, we can attribute these symptoms and quirks to one gender more readily. Many exceptions exist for the type of quirks attributed to either gender, too, of course. For example, in some relationships, husbands are more decisive and bossy than their wives. Yet, decisiveness and bossiness tendencies can be detected more often amongst wives. The prevalence of, and wide variations in, these tendencies also have a lot to do with culture and environment.

In all, the main point is that, in almost all relationships, one spouse has a higher tendency in the twenty quirks that are noted in the following pages as manly or womanly. Due to the low level of teamwork in relationships, almost all relationships suffer from spouses' tendencies in the twenty symptoms noted for men and women. Usually, one spouse is bossier, one spouse is needier, one spouse is grouchier, one spouse is more sensitive, etc. As long as differences in the level of some or all these tendencies are noticeable, real and perceived quirks erupt and affect relationships. Nevertheless, the collection of twenty general quirks suggested in this book for men and women are quite typical in most relationships.

It must be also reiterated that the end purpose of all the discussions regarding gender quirks is only to raise couples' awareness about the nature of the most prevalent obstacles in relationships. Accordingly, the objective is to encourage more teamwork, understanding, and sympathy between partners in a relationship. The point is definitely not to criticize or condemn the peculiar qualities/quirks of any gender.

Women's qualities and quirks are listed again below for discussing each item in some detail.

Women's Qualities & Symptoms Appearing as Quirks

Quality	leading to	Quirk
1. Decisiveness	→	Bossiness/inflexibility
2. Activeness	→	Frustration/impatience
3. Neatness	→	Fussiness/stressful
4. Seeking Independence	→	Need more dependence
5. Optimism	→	Shortsightedness
6. Strong Identity	→	Resilience/bonding
7. Motherhood	→	Lesser role for men
8. Seeking Love	→	Romanticism/hopeful
9. High MLove	→	Release emotions
10. Seeking Adventure	→	Disgruntled

Decisiveness → Bossiness/inflexibility

Decisiveness is indeed a high quality in our culture, nowadays. Yet, our naïve (or selfish) intentions and urges for decisiveness cause havoc in relationships, instead of emerging as a quality. In fact, it is often imprudent to make a decision without great caution and our partner's cooperation. For one thing, the level of accuracy of information needed for every decision makes the matter of being a good decision maker quite hard and risky these days. Therefore, being decisive means trouble if a person erroneously assumes that s/he has all the necessary data, or a sacred foresight, for making a decision. Second, our intuition and emotions usually mislead us regarding the proper decision criteria needed for making the right choices. Third, our tone of voice and approach when stating our decisions might radiate arrogance that can destroy the effect of any decision even if it were a useful one. Fourth, we must always leave lots of room about our assumptions and decisions being wrong. The worst enemy of decisiveness is human's dogmatism and tendency to trust our analysis, decision criteria, and conclusions.

The *Doubts and Decisions for Living* trilogy explains the perils of decision-making and people's certitude regarding their ideas. (See the list of the author's books at the beginning of the book.) Certitude that drives most of our decisiveness attempts is merely a sign of naiveté, stubbornness, and arrogance, and not a personal quality. In all, without maintaining some level of doubts regarding our viewpoints, our decisiveness is more a source of problem for ourselves and others than a life quality. Then, when it turns into a habit of bossiness and inflexibility, the silliness of the situation and the damage it inflicts on our relationships become obvious.

Naturally, the practical purpose of our doubts is to keep our guard in society and avoid making hasty decisions and getting hurt. However, as a finer personal purpose, maintaining some degree of doubts helps us keep our sanity and humility, since certitude merely makes us dogmatic, arrogant, and stubborn. Without our 'doubts,' we do not exploit the opportunity for self-awareness. Without our positive 'doubts' we forget how insignificant we humans are in the large scheme of Creation and the universe. Without our 'doubts,' we would be even less instinctual and natural. And without some doubts about the existing social structure and values, we would never look for an alternative lifestyle, in which our attitudes and minds are not manipulated, our Egos and sense of superiority are not boosted senselessly, and our lives are not so shallow and aimless.

In all, women's decisiveness mostly reflects their reliance on their intuition (which imposes a definite point of view), but also the influence of their strong Model telling them that being indecisive is unattractive. Yet, decisiveness makes women less patient and more stubborn with their positions or opinions. Then, they are also sensitive and become defensive when their decisions and viewpoints are not understood or not acted upon immediately.

Active → Frustration/impatience

All the items on the list of women's qualities play a major role in making women active, sometimes to the verge of obsession. They are too active for keeping the household in shipshape, neat and organized. They are active to implement the barrage of decisions they make nonstop and to make sure the expected results are achieved. They are active to prove and maintain their independence, to boost their identity, to perform their maternal role most diligently, to find love, etc. And if all these activities are not enough to keep them busy and satiate their obsessions, they are quite adventurous and choosy about how things should be done, which create a lot more concern and activity for them. Their 'optimism,' as another quality on the list, makes them hopeful that they can achieve all these goals and perform all these activities. Accordingly, they are bound to face as many obstacles related to the large number of goals and activities they are contemplating and following at any point. Therefore, they often get frustrated and impatient when things do not happen as quickly or orderly as they wish.

Despite their vast action orientation, women are not as much proactive in the sense of planning rather long-term and strategically. They are less proactive than they are pro activity. Even then, the type of activities they are keen about, especially order and cleanliness, is the least valued by men. In fact, these activities often appear like a big, noisy hoopla that cause more nuisance than add substantive value. As men often perceive all these extra activities as quirks, women get testy and frustrated for being criticized, instead of appreciated for all their *special* efforts.

Neat and organized → Fussiness/stressful

For most women, there is no limit for neatness, organization, and order. The only problem is that not enough time is in a day to get everything they imagine necessary done!

I just cannot stop myself from quoting a real story that happened to me a few years ago during my first visit with a woman whom I had known from a distance, but never had a chance to live with (all after my divorce, of course!) When I visited her in her city of residence far away from mine, she asked (or rather ordered) me to wipe the water off the tiles surrounding the bathtub after every shower, the same way she did it herself. Between the two of us, we cleaned those tiles 2-4 times every day. She just could not bear the sight of the wet tiles, I guess. Her fussiness was directed not merely at the poor tiles, but also other stuff that did not need my participation in cleanliness (thank god), especially that early in the morning!

I really liked her, though! She was highly educated, kind, beautiful, and had a great career. Therefore, when I returned to Vancouver after three weeks, I was quite eager to call her and ask her to marry me even though I was the one who had to move to a new city, so that she could keep her job. A writer can do his work anywhere, presumably. 'Fine,' I told myself, 'she is worth all my efforts.' However, I realized that I really could not clean the tiles after every shower for the rest of my life. I considered explaining my dilemma or even confronting her about the matter. Yet, it was clear that she would either get upset for refusing to do a simple thing she was asking me to do for her or resent me for having to do my job herself after my showers, since she seemed adamant about water-free tiles. Such a cynical person I have turned into, nowadays, I had also imagined the likelihood of she telling me very nicely not to worry about the tiles if I had raised the issue until…! *Until we got married and she insisted after a couple of days or so that I must begin doing my share of tile cleaning from then on...!!*

On the one hand, I hope she never reads, or hears about, my comments here regarding her cleanliness obsession. On the other hand, I hope she does, so that she realizes that the only reason I did not marry her, despite my tremendous love and respect for her. Just in case you are curious, I should say yes, she had told me she loved me, too! Sorry...!

This episode surely reflects one of the extreme cases. Yet, this high quality in most women for order and cleanliness is just precious, except for causing unsettling dilemmas like the one I faced in the above story. In most relationships, some level of pressure is placed on both partners due to the women's need for order and cleanliness. *I could've had a perfect wife if only she wasn't so crazy about the tiles!* At the other extreme, when a woman has no obsession with order and cleanliness, usually (but not always) the outcome is a complete catastrophe in terms of disorder and carelessness, even about the basic sense of hygiene. *Sadly, I have experienced that myself, too! Worse, I might have sounded like a womanizer, arrogant, or crazy man. Then again, I might have been merely an unlucky person with my share of weird stories about women!!!*

Seek independence → Need more dependence

The most evident result of the new social setting and women's progressive role in professional life is the complications of our needs for both independence and dependence personally and in relationships. We need both independence and dependence, but creating a right balance has become quite complex in the new social setting. This matter is explained in Chapter Seven. It might help to read that section now, if you wish. Here, the only point to emphasize is that women's new social role goads them to look for more independence to affirm their identity, while deep down need more dependence and support due to their emotional and MLove tendencies. At the same time, the effect of all the changes in women's life in the new era might gradually diminish their emotional tendencies and need for dependence that has been customary so far. The outcome of the qualities and symptoms listed for women at the beginning of this chapter, especially their strong identity, resilience, bonding, decisiveness, and other qualities and symptoms, has already changed some women's mentalities, including a lesser need for dependence. A large group is emerging, nowadays, in political and corporate careers with exceptional capacities to outdo men in all social roles due to the combination of all the above noted qualities and symptoms. They can pursue and achieve such high objectives only due to their ability to control their need for dependence on others in order to focus better on their careers and ambitions. A large percentage of women may gradually build an equal level of tenacity for self-actualization and success in the future. However, at this point, the majority still has a high need for dependence, while satisfying it in new relationships has become tough and frustrating for them. The reason is that men and women cannot balance their needs for both dependence and independence either personally or in their relationships.

Optimistic → Shortsightedness

Optimism makes women less conscious and concerned about the real sources of conflicts in relationships, including the one noted above about the difficulty of aligning our independence and dependence needs either personally or in our relationships. Shortsightedness is a by-product of optimism, which hinders people's abilities to see and accept the flaws with their present mentalities about relationships. Instead, they strive to achieve their goals, including happiness and love, according to some unrealistic assumptions and criteria. The effects of these social and mental obstacles on family relationships are often negative and worrisome, as explained in Part III.

Strong identity → Resilience/bonding

No doubt, women have built a strong identity for themselves, at least in their minds and presentations. We witness specific tactics and ideologies that they spread in their interactions. They have built an even deeper resilience due to their ability to bond and share their plans, success stories, and hurts. In line with women's eagerness for high independence, the stronger their identity becomes, the more it might alienate them from men. This mayhem will grow every year if a new mechanism for gender interactions and marriages are not developed soon and accepted by most of us.

Maternal → Lesser role for men

As if women's emerging strong identity were not alienating men enough already, women's instincts, when mixed with life pressures and priorities, make them somewhat casual about men's needs. Instead, they focus on their children during the limited time they have in their busy daily lives. The symptoms of women's decisiveness and need for organizing the family affair quickly and effectively further restricts men's role and participation in family choices and routines. Therefore, men feel less included in the family decisions and not receiving enough respect around the house.

Seek love → Romanticism/hopeful

Despite all the above points about women's drive for identity and independence, and despite the emerging perception about their insensitivity towards men's needs, deep down they are not only quite sensitive, but also oversensitive too often. Their optimism, mixed with the effects of movies raising their drive for romanticism in the new culture, has made women hopeful about conquering love and tasting romance, while they like to enjoy their sexual freedom, too! The inner conflict they have caused for themselves due to the low likelihood of reconciling their needs for both love and sex in the same relationship (or several relationships) over a long time is another big source of mayhem in marital relationships.

Women are noted to be 'emotional.' The reasons are that they are vastly driven by their instincts and they have better control of Model. They can charm or even shed tears naturally to influence others. On the other hand, men are less capable of being charming or manipulative due to their allegedly logical minds and higher arrogance. Reliance on Model and intuition clearly makes women so emotional and vulnerable. Thus, they have been forced to build some type of defence mechanism to make up for the risks of their oversensitivity—by becoming a bit more practical than they are by nature. To do so, they have become more suspicious, calculating, and clever. This need has made them alert and eager to devise preventative steps for protecting themselves. This is another good reason for them to become assertive. Then, when they push the limits, this crude assertiveness often leads to aggressiveness, because the art of being assertive is not easy to master.

On the other hand, women's sensitivity leads to their higher expectations from relationships. They expect their husbands to grasp their needs better, comply readily, etc. Since men are not equipped to realize and respond properly, in a timely manner, to this oversensitivity, more clashes and retaliations erupt in relationships. In fact, men cannot understand why women are so sensitive and react to simplest inconveniences in such a harsh manner. Women come across as too demanding and complaining, nowadays, because of their raw oversensitivity.

High MLove → Release emotions

On the one hand, women's ability to release their emotions helps them cope with family commotions and disappointments in society. Their attempts to at least share their hurts with one another help them immensely. On the other hand, men's and society's low capacities to respond to women's sentiments feels frustrating and it becomes a cause for frictions in relationships.

Women are more emotional partially due to their higher levels of the three love components, i.e., ELove, MLove, and SLove, again due to their instinctual urges. However, they are emotional also because they know better how to use MLove to express love better than men can. Men have little or no MLove aptitude, but they are equally suffering from the deprivations caused by their unfulfilled ELove and SLove. Men's natural resistance (due to their logical tendency) towards MLove often frustrates them, too. Yet, not as much as it frustrates women, who do not understand why their MLove remains unanswered, and why men are so incapable of MLove—romance.

Adventurous/choosy → Disgruntled

Women's craving for love and happiness naturally makes them more adventurous and choosy in order to make the best of life options and their times. Accordingly, they have grown high standards and expectations from life and relationships. Then again, life's realities hardly respond to all those dreams. Thus, women feel disgruntled, which in turn goads them to become more anxious and adventurous. This vicious cycle causes deep inner conflicts and turmoil for them. The result is that women take twice as much antidepressant to keep going in society and coping. Surely, the effect of their optimism and misperceptions about life infect the health of relationships, too.

The effects of all these qualities and symptoms is apparent in the strong, peculiar *identity* that women portray in society, nowadays, and we can notice and feel it in all aspects of life as well. It is plausible that our value systems, including social mannerism and culture, are mostly a reflection of what women like. The reason is that women are the ones who support the ideas and customs within their households, but also across the society and nations by propagating them among themselves most effectively. They are choosier regarding all values and norms. They are decisive, active, powerful around the family, manipulative, organizer, adventurous, intuitive, with immense charm, maternal instincts, MLove, and a strong identity that they keep pushing its boundaries. What stronger force could there be in the universe for shaping the customs and desires of the poor human population?

By the way, women's approach and ambitions fit extremely nicely with the goals of capitalism. Therefore, they get support from all the men and forces pushing capitalism to the extreme. Therefore, women have the ultimate power and responsibility of pondering the risks of current culture and the repercussion of not making humans (especially men) revamp their visions and plans for humanity. Women have the chance to prevent so much suffering for the future generations (their children) if we merely stayed the course and followed our current demented mentalities about existence and our planet.

Sorry for preaching!

Studying the passive, submissive qualities of men in the next chapter supports the idea of women's influence on shaping the characteristics of new societies even further. This might be a positive revelation for redirecting the destiny of humanity and saving the planet from too much egoism, destruction, and greed that society has inflicted upon itself so far with its wars, religions, political and economic systems under men's rule. On the other hand, if women's success makes them as egotistical and uncompassionate as men, then the future of human culture becomes even more complicated and doubtful, especially if all these changes keep alienating men and women, while melting the foundation of families, too.

CHAPTER SIX
Manly Quirks

Men's ten qualities and related symptoms are precious in their own ways, but contradict women's almost line-by-line. Thus, their roles in causing relationship clashes and personal inner conflicts are rather obvious. However, couples are not conscious about, or even familiar, with these basic facts about gender qualities and symptoms.

Men's Qualities & Symptoms Appearing as Quirks

Quality	leading to	Symptom
1. Pensive	→	Doubtfulness/indecisiveness
2. Passive	→	Submissiveness/laziness
3. Loose/Natural	→	Sloppiness/inattentiveness
4. Seeking dependence	→	Need more independence
5. Realistic in general	→	Less needy
6. Poor Identity	→	Confusion/frustration
7. Creative	→	Seclusion
8. Low trust in love	→	Inability to relate
9. Low MLove	→	Pent-up emotions
10. Content	→	Unresponsiveness

These qualities and symptoms, which are emerging and acting as relationship quirks, are reviewed briefly in this chapter.

Pensive → Doubtfulness/indecisiveness

Obviously, everybody tries to use logic and patience to make better decisions, instead of solely relying on intuition or letting haste take the best of him or her. However, men do it a little bit more than it seems necessary to women. It is plausible that men have always faced a wider range of external forces and threats than women have. Thus, they have gained a higher 'logic orientation' than women, too. Conversely, women might have remained in closer contact with their instincts due to their maternal urges. Yet, intuition does not always provide the best answers for the problems of modern societies. Instincts were good tools for primitive humans. Many of those instincts are still good guides for us, sometimes. Yet, many of our innate urges are no longer effective for handling all sorts of artificial parameters and values introduced into our daily lives. These days, instincts alone cannot respond to complex situations in society. And our logic, which men like to depend on a lot, is often contaminated by Ego, anyway.

We can escape neither our doubts, nor the need for making decisions. Planning our lives is an intuitive urge for intelligent people, however our success depends on how well we analyse our options, doubts, and decision factors in a timely manner. Making the right choices in life is a complex task, especially since we suspect the reliability of information, social structure, and human nature. On the one hand, being proactive is getting more urgent daily, considering our dynamic—and confusing—socioeconomic environment and the growing contamination of information base. On the other hand, we should understand the true nature and importance of our doubts for managing our decisions objectively and patiently, while also making sure our doubts do not cause more mental stagnation or procrastination.

This type of mentality about the difficulty of life choices is more prevalent among men—as historical breadwinners—thus they are more pensive and cautious. Men's apprehension feels, especially, too drastic compared with women who depend on their intuition, optimism, and a sense of adventure to take life in their strides more readily. More women are willing to live in the now than worrying about the repercussions of wrong decisions. Men are usually more doubtful about their actions and decisions, because they are more risk averse and rely on their raw logic for decision-making. This is true even though they have higher Ego and an urge to come across as decisive. Logic always requires an assessment of alternatives, which causes delays and uncertainty.

The reason women complain more often than men is also related to their tendency for fast, intuitive decision making and low patience for men to overanalyse seemingly urgent projects or procrastinate (due to their contemplation habits), especially since women usually feel restless about most decisions, which by the way should be fully to their liking as well!

Passive → Submissiveness/laziness

Men are rather passive due to their life outlook and realistic impressions of social values and interactions. Yet, they appear even more passive and lazy to women, which would then lead to family frictions. Two of the important points noted on Page 14 about gender qualities and quirks must be reiterated here as support for men's passivity:

1. Each gender quality and its symptoms are related to other personality attributes (qualities and quirks) noted for that gender. For example, men's passivity is the outcome of their cautious mind, loose nature, realism, poor identity, etc. Accordingly, people cannot change their personality attributes readily even if they agreed they were destructive for them or their relationships.
2. Although genders' high qualities and symptoms irritate the opposite gender, without such disparity people would have tortured one another and ruined their relationships even

> further. Just imagine both genders being equally decisive and active based on their intuitions, or were both passive. Not only more frictions would have erupted all the time between partners, but also their life routines would have become even more risky without at least some general checks and balances that the present gender differences impose on relationships. *God knew what He was doing!*

Thus, men's passivity should be considered a blessing in some respects, too, while the irritation and frictions resulting form it cannot be lightly ignored, either. Besides, men are most likely not passive by choice. Rather, it is often due to the forces of nature and society keeping men flexible, in hopes of fulfilling their need for dependence on a woman to some extent.

Loose/Natural → Sloppiness/inattention

Men are preoccupied merely by their immediate needs, with less fanaticism, optimism, and adaptation aptitude. Thus, they have become relatively looser and more natural than women are. Women value social fad and etiquette and get influenced by commercials and fashion faster. Therefore, men look rather crude, sloppy, and inattentive to women. Now, the question is which approach reflects and serves human nature and society better. Is it wise to become phonier due to consumerism and showy lifestyles or try to keep as much of our naturalness as possible, although it makes men look sloppy and inattentive? Is life worth getting too hung-up over so many artificial needs and ambitions? Should we really keep propagating our phony lifestyles as a raw symbol of progress and modernism?

Seek dependence → Need more independence

It sounds illogical to say that someone seeks dependence when he actually needs independence. Thus, it must be clarified that everybody needs both dependence and independence, in some rotating priority, nowadays. We have lower needs, such as food and shelter, to fulfil first, nowadays, before directing our efforts towards satisfying higher needs like status or love. We all like to satisfy our higher needs, since they give us a better sense of tranquility and self-worth. For men, in particular, the need for dependence is a lower need and independence is a higher one. Thus, for satisfying their need for independence, men should first fulfil their dependence need, which comes mostly from companionship. Yet, satisfying this basic need is getting too complex and difficult for them, because keeping a mate requires so many sacrifices and concessions against their nature and their higher, precious need for independence.

For women, the order is typically reversed, because they value love and compassion that comes from dependence and companionship, and because they need support to fulfil their highly potent maternal need and to raise their offspring. In fact, women's need for independence has mostly emerged in recent decades as they began striving for individualism and equality merely to establish a new identity for themselves.

In a sense, we can say that women's need for independence and men's need for dependence are newly developed needs, which are rather superficial like many other needs that the new social structure has planted in people's minds as new priorities.

Realistic → Less needy

Overall, men seem more realistic about life and its meaning than women are. Women are much more eager to define the meaning of life to enjoy every moment of their lives the best they can. However, men seem to have settled somehow better about the fact that life has no specific meaning; thus putting expectations on it would be a waste of energy on raw whims and adventures that only cause frustration. They are content with a simpler lifestyle, although they keep working hard and follow their ambitions mostly to feel successful and have a better chance of finding the right kind of women for marriage.

Poor identity → Confusion/frustration

As much as they try to impress women and keep them happy without losing their own integrity and self-image too much, men have only faced more resistance and rejection, since their qualities and mentalities no longer match those of women's or the ones that women seek in a man. The outcome is obvious. Men have no *manhood or family* identity, while pressured by women's strong (but crude) identity that keeps expanding with no plan for bringing men and women together mentally.

Thus, for the time being, men's confusion and frustration from the existing undefined means of gender communication would continue to hurt both their wives and their relationships.

Creative → Seclusion

The more men seek dependence and feel more deprived of it, the more mental seclusion they sense and face. Meanwhile, women's maternal quality and attachment to their children make the matter worse when men find lesser importance in family, while women focus on children. Women's sense of high achievement in the creation and care of their children fulfils their high-level personal needs largely, but also pushes men into mental and physical seclusion. Therefore, some smarter men use the occasion to be somehow creative in their own ways, although they might feel they cannot compete with women in that regard, either. Still, they try their best to seek creativity for amusing themselves. Maybe they could impress women with their creativity, too! Those less creative men try to find other means of filling this gap in their lives, which would be some significant form of creativity in itself merely for coping with the *absurd reality of living* in the absence of sensible purposes for existence and new relationships.

Low trust in love → Inability to relate

Men's inability to relate is not fully their fault. They have just become this way—so untrusting—due to their experiences and cultural influence. They feel odd about the whole matter, too. Therefore, we should remember this fact when we assess the circumstances and symptoms of men's and women's traits (qualities) interacting and making both genders sceptical about the other gender's odd qualities, the meaning of love, partners' sincerity, relationships, commitment, trust, etc. In the final analysis, the way men and women feel and behave is nobody's fault. The only problem is that nobody seems to be looking for real solutions and redefining relationships more in line with the new personal and social mentalities.

Low MLove → Pent-up emotions

Due to their higher passivity and looseness (living somewhat naturally) in general, men's Model is less developed. Thus, they look rather crude compared to women who have adopted social norms heartily and adapted themselves rather perfectly. Men supposedly get together and bond, too, but their efforts are not deep and reliable in the way women are so good on this matter as well.

Accordingly, men usually have no or very little MLove to begin with due to their lower potentiality for Model or even perceiving (validating) love. Therefore, they know less about stirring up, or responding to, romance. Then, they suffer more also at the time of separation due to their lower adaptability to change and relationship failure, again due to their lower Model and higher Ego. Lower capacity for Mlove also diminishes men's ability to align their ELove and SLove needs (or using their MLove to make up for the lack of ELove and SLove).

Content → Unresponsiveness

With all the symptoms and effects of men's qualities noted in this chapter, it is easy to see why men have been (appear) so preoccupied and somewhat content with basic facts of life. They appear unresponsive to women's demand for adventure, more romance, and compliance. The only question is whether the matter will keep getting worse and out of hand eventually, or men can change themselves to women's liking. On the other hand, maybe both genders come to their senses and realize that only through teamwork and practical mentalities they can minimize the level of frictions in relationships.

We cannot stop wondering about the dire effects of emerging gender differences on the direction of human life. Are these new gender differences partly biological or mostly conditional due to our modern thinking? How are they going to change us and our relationships in the future? These topics are beyond the scope of this book. Yet, it seems reasonable, for example, to expect MLove increasing in men in the future after several decades of proper exposure to environments that might boost such a need in them in an authentic manner. They must build up some minimal trust gradually first, though, instead of being forced to play certain roles without deep conviction. Whether the situation in relationships would improve enough to bolster trust between men and women is a big question, though.

PART III

Gender Quarrels

CHAPTER SEVEN
Gender Sensitive Personal Needs

Human qualities and quirks cause them a large variety of dilemmas and hurdles in relationships, as noted in previous chapters. Ironically, the roots of these obstacles and the effects of gender differences are related to our crude personal needs and perceptions in line with our vain culture and social values provoking humans' crooked nature. Accordingly, realizing the role of the following **Ten Personal Needs** thru self-awareness can improve our relationships vastly:

1. Happiness
2. Love
3. Sex
4. Equality
5. Individualism
6. Fairness
7. Control
8. Manipulation/Domination
9. Dependence
10. Independence

These needs feel like logical expectations for healthy persons living in a modern society. We strive to satisfy these needs in order to maximize our lives' values or defend ourselves against the growing evil in society. Yet, deep emotional conflicts arise and many obstacles ruin relationships when couples' struggles for the same need, such as happiness, affect their perceptions of each other and their relationships' health. The above ten personal needs are particularly gender sensitive in the way they affect partners' expectations from relationships and life in different, bizarre manners according to their genders. So many gender quarrels relate to partners' misperceptions of these ten critical needs, thus they are explained in length in this chapter to raise couples' awareness and sensitivity.

Need for Happiness

Happiness is a myth all by itself, but expecting relationships to provide it is too idealistic. We have difficulty even defining it, as it is not a stable state or experience. Yet, we like to perceive it as a lasting state of joy and tranquility, which we also expect to result from our endless materialistic desires, competitions, greed, and shoddy relationships. This is a big conflict already. We want happiness to fit our crooked, materialistic lifestyles, rather than a lifestyle that can stir peace of mind as the closest state of happiness. Instead, happiness needs a big change of mindset and lifestyle (mainly towards selflessness), which only a few of us might eventually find the courage to adopt.

Anyhow, partners expect each other and their relationship to fulfil their illusory perceptions of happiness, including their egotistical and materialistic needs, pleasure, sexuality, and lasting tranquility. This expectation is actually one major cause of relationship breakdowns. Partners deprive themselves from the basic privileges of relationships, since they naively believe relationships are meant to bring them some kind of magical happiness. They cause themselves and each other pain with their obsessions for happiness through relationships. We have imposed this ironic condition on ourselves in recent decades. Moreover, it seems that with women's new progressive role in society, they are now seeking happiness too actively, while expecting men to play a bigger role than before in finding happiness for them.

Meanwhile, everybody has lost sight of the only possible path for happiness. That is, instead of learning selflessness and contentment to empower their inner 'self' and relationships, people strive to strengthen their crude identities in society and relationships through arrogance, then expect happiness, too! In that sense, society and relationships create the best settings for the wicked aspects of human nature to erupt and cause distress and despair rather than happiness. Accordingly, gender clashes are also rising due to couple's misperceptions about happiness and its role in relationships.

In fact, human nature does not support happiness and peace due to humans' innate urges for challenge, power, controversy, domination, competition, greed, struggle for survival, etc. In fact, anger, hatred, jealousy, spite, and aggressiveness come to us naturally, but we must try hard to be honest, compassionate, genuine, and all the other good stuff required for developing happiness. Life is not a happy journey, either. Our occasional taste of happiness and peace soon dissolves as new dilemmas and disappointments overwhelm us. Therefore, as the first step towards tranquility, and also improving our relationships, we must learn that happiness is a myth and not a stable state. Only if we gain some sacred wisdom and maturity, we may succeed in grasping a sense of contentment, thru self-awareness, which provides the closest manifestation of lasting happiness.

As another misperception, most of us mistake pleasures (e.g., sexuality) with happiness, or assume that more pleasures lead to happiness. Thus, most relationships become instable soon, only because they fail to satisfy our fantastic appetite for pleasure and sexuality. Surely, we cannot avoid the impression that companionship can fulfil a large number of our personal needs. However, relying on others or relationships to satisfy our personal needs and bring us happiness is naïve and the leading cause of our pains. Any chance for tasting this elusive happiness is to seek it within ourselves based on our mental ability and awareness. Mostly, we must relieve our marriages from our demands to bring us happiness on top of satisfying a large array of our sundry personal needs and life deprivations.

Happiness is a complex topic for discussion, especially within the context of our crooked social values. Many books are written about this topic and maybe another one is due to explain the connection between happiness and relationships in more details than are possible in this book. Of course, the natural conclusion in most 'happiness' books is that it may be found only inside a person and he/she needs a special mindset to grasp and reach that state. This is what this author advocates as well with an emphasis on becoming better humans through self-awareness, to contact our spirits and resist many artificial facets of life in the new era. Yet, this book stresses on staying practical and grasping our humanly limitations, which obstruct our efforts to be content and a better person. A collection of happiness definitions can be reviewed in *On Happiness*, by Nima Omidi, Perennial Books, 2014. This author's book, *the Mysteries of Life, Love, and Happiness*, is also a good source.

Some books (quoting philosophers, Buddhism, and the Dalai Lama) suggest that life's purpose is to find happiness. This notion seems rather simplistic, since life has no purpose per se; yet especially, life has no capacity or intention to offer happiness to humans. We humans have many other ambitions besides happiness. The purpose of life (within the context of creation) is neither to spread happiness, nor to create good humans, judging by humans' historical attitude. Happiness cannot even be conceived as one's life purpose (regardless of the purpose of the universe). Life is just a collection of events and moments that transpires in people's lives based on natural laws and luck, and affects them based on their cognition (i.e., awareness, intelligence, beliefs, etc.). Sorry Dalai Lama!

We usually perceive happiness as an antidote for suffering. We all prefer happiness mostly because suffering hurts and not that it is the life's purpose. We often pursue many ambitions in life with greater passion than our desire for happiness or even pleasures, e.g., need for love, power, or recognition. Most of us just cannot sit idle and be happy with our contentment. We hate boredom and we want adventures even if they cause pain. We want to be loved, although it often leads to disappointment and pain. The point is that we are not born to be happy or good humans and these are not the purposes of life. We *might* want to become better beings to soothe our hurts, release tension, or prefer (or like to pretend) to be at peace with ourselves and our surroundings. Happiness and goodness are probable outcomes of our personal choices to set the right balance between our ambitions and contentment. Life has no special meaning, nor is it about anything special. Even if life is about something or has a meaning, God has not yet revealed it to us through His prophets, nor has He given us enough intelligence to figure it out personally.

The slogan 'life is for the purpose of happiness' is actually causing more suffering than guiding people towards happiness. The reason is that it makes people believe that such a myth (happiness) really exists, and that the only reason they cannot capture it is due to their stupidity or relationships. Thus, they feel useless and anxious. They abandon their relationships prematurely or seek all kinds of pleasures and sexuality in hopes of fulfilling the alleged purpose of life, i.e., happiness. But then, they feel even more empty and lost. Happiness has now turned into an advertising tool with hypnotic effects on common, naive people.

Most importantly, life is not for the purpose of getting hung up over a mythical concept like happiness and causing extra suffering for ourselves and our spouses. Almost nobody can find that elusive happiness. The one percent who claims to have found it, like monks and sages, must make big sacrifices, limit their social activities, and accept celibacy and suffering in order to maintain their state of contentment, which they call happiness. Happiness appears to demand a lot of selflessness, celibacy, sacrifice, meditation, solitude, and sacred sufferings. Yet, by nature, most of us are selfish, and love our sexuality and pleasures, which would accordingly lead to unhappiness.

How many of us are willing to be celibate, limit our pleasures and social lives, and welcome pain to reach enlightenment (for happiness)? We have to force ourselves truly to fulfil most of these requirements, which shows happiness could never be a natural pursuit of humans, especially in a materialistic world. Accordingly, the purpose of our existence is not to look for happiness, as the Dalai Lama says, because we humans are not prepared to pay the price for it and we are not made for it. It is possible that he is referring to 'contentment,' yet it is essential to distinguish happiness from contentment. Seeking happiness might be a wrong strategy for many of us, indeed, as it appears to be against our nature. To find peace and contentment, we must grow as a being naturally. We must think and act within our natural capacities, while aiming to be better human beings, too. In particular, blaming our relationships and partners for not inducing the happiness that we cannot find anywhere else on our own is a silly attitude prevalent in society, nowadays.

The fact that we seek happiness all our lives in vain reveals our inner turmoil and inability to signify our existence within simpler terms personally. The fact that we have to try so hard to become better persons shows that humans are not pure by nature. It also reveals our stubbornness to accept our inherent debility as humans, which could be the first step for building personal humility towards enlightenment. On the other hand, acknowledging our impurity could motivate us to overcome our Egos and try harder to grasp the meaning and process of becoming better beings—not as a social ideal per se, but just because it would make us happier at the end. The simple fact that Ego is an inherent part of human psyche is enough to cause human bias, selfishness, hypocrisy, malice, and hundreds of other flaws. The fact that we are so greedy and competitive, and the way we cherish capitalism, materialism, and pleasures shows that we are impure by nature. The fact that Christians believe Jesus died because of people's sins—and similar beliefs in other religions—shows humans' tendency to sin. The fact that so many relationships fail nowadays, and the way partners treat each other like dirt at the time of separation, shows their impurity. It also shows people's inabilities to get along and show compassion. The fact that we must constantly go for confessions and repentance, to cleanse our suffering souls, is another clue about human impurity. The fact that we do good things and charity as well (often for self-serving purposes, to clean our conscience, or for pretences) does not wash all other negative tendencies that exist in human nature. Naturally, we cannot find happiness until we resolve all these shortcomings of being a human and learn to get along more civilly. Maybe life, love, and happiness are linked in very peculiar ways, and maybe we can solve these three mysteries together someday, after all! It is just a matter of developing the wisdom of seeing the sacred truth outside the modern social norms.

The success of a relationship depends on the goodness of its partners—and humans' nature overall. Yet, people's attitude and nature indicate that the chance of creating even a small society of pure humans is slim, as they would not be allowed to choose and live as they like against social norms. Actually, it is easier to prove that humans become more arrogant and unreliable as time goes by and gender differences grow, too. Thus, it gets harder for people (especially opposite genders) to get along in relationships and society and behold happiness. Developing a pure man within the crooked values of modern society simply feels like a funny concept. It sounds like a plan to nurture edible fish in a polluted swamp. With the speed we are ruining the environment, where nature is meant to flourish itself and embrace us, too, how could a puritan emerge? How could anybody capture happiness within this social chaos?

Need for Love

Couples have become too romantic, but also too antagonistic in the recent decades. Everybody, especially women, believe that love must be the foundation of relationships. In this sense, life has become a big theatre. Everybody tries to be romantic. And they expect their partners to be equally good in romance, too, as a test of their commitment. Yet, they retaliate harshly, and reveal their evil sides, when love fades away—which happens regularly in most relationships. They turn separation into such a calamity when they realize that their supposedly initial love had been a farce. They make their partners' and own lives hell because love has evaporated (if there had been any real love to begin with). Now couples turn into ferocious adversaries accusing each other of lying about their love promises at the outset. They curse their partners for not loving them anymore, as though love were something to force upon oneself and not a natural feeling. And they find their partners responsible for the lost love, even if they are the ones feeling out of love. Actually, they usually blame their partners for making them fall out of love. They accuse their partners of having killed their love. They also blame them for their loss of youth. These past lovers now suddenly view each other as criminals deserving a severe punishment, including a difficult and costly separation. The penalty for falling out of love is too horrendous, nowadays. Thus, some people—especially men—keep playing the role of a romantic fool to keep the situation under control. They take the humiliation of submitting to their spouses' whims to stop their whining, and since the penalties, financially and emotionally, for ending relationships are high.

As noted in Chapter Three, the gender gap and conflicts are widening due to people's—especially women's—assumptions about love. For one thing, women have a higher aptitude for, and misperceptions about, all three types of love, i.e., Slove, Elove, and Mlove compared with men. This difference causes many misunderstanding and gender quarrels. Moreover, while women are getting keener to use love as a relationship success factor, men are losing their trust in love, especially since they are instinctually and culturally less inclined to be romantic and sensitive enough for women's liking. Men and women are so incompatible overall that when they match and live together permanently, it appears like a magical and spiritual revelation beyond our normal (expected) worldly experiences. It is such an odd event and coincidence. Still we naïvely believe it must happen to most of us, so we pursue it as a sensible expectation. In all, learning more about the nature of love and people's mentality about it can help reduce genders' clashes.

Almost everybody finally admits that love, in the manner they had initially imagined it, is a transitory state. Then, they may decide that the option of staying in loveless relationships, against their convictions, is preferable to loneliness or high penalties of separation. However, they—especially women—now do not know how to handle a relationship that is not driven by love. They believe their relationship has failed and has no value. Some may seek love in another person's arms; to find the passion they believe they deserve.

Everybody believes s/he deserves love and must find it somehow. Yet, we all ignore a simple fact about the basic sole implication of love: That the more one seeks SLove, the more one must be honest and reliable in character, which is getting more difficult these days because of all the games introduced in relationships. Of course, we think we can hide our mistrust, hypocrisy, and dishonesty from the rest of the world, which merely shows our arrogance and trust in Model to bail us out. The good news is that people can largely see each other's true nature despite all the elaborate games they play to portray a false personality of themselves and to conceal their calculating nature. In all, the games and retaliations in relationships reveal how silly the notion of gauging the strength of our marriages by love is. We simply ignore all these contradictions and keep looking for SLove in such a confusing environment.

The matter of resolving our relationship conundrums have become too complex in this convoluted social setting as well. On the one hand, getting out of our relationships is usually excruciating, in terms of the hassles imposed by our partners and society (the judicial system in particular). On the other hand, many couples are frustrated and confused, nowadays, because they feel trapped in their loveless (usually hostile) relationships. The situation is in particular stressful for persons who truly believe that love is the core of relationships. Even worse, many couples have to continue playing some phony roles that marriage counsellors recommend in order to save their relationships.

Our present mindset reflects our lack of clarity about the nature of love and its limited role in relationships. We have burdened our relationships and our psyches by insisting that relationships must be justified and driven by love. In fact, the contemporary definition of relationships within our confusing culture permeates many invalid myths. We believe that:

- Love is the test of success for relationships.
- Love lasts forever.
- Love makes a relationship last forever.
- Relationships must be validated by love.
- Relationships thrive on love.
- Anybody considering a serious relationship should and would find a person to exchange love with each other.
- Expressing love regularly ensures relationships' success.
- Love is a common phenomenon that everyone recognizes and is capable of delivering.
- Love is a common commodity that everyone must find and enjoy in his/her life.
- When there is love, relationship problems are rare and manageable.
- Love overcomes all the relationship problems.
- Partners have control over their feelings to love each other forever.
- Etc.

These myths are incongruent with the nature of relationships, especially in the new era where people are so self-centred and calculating. Love does not have the meaning or the power stipulated in the above myths. Nor do relationships necessarily last longer if partners start theirs mostly based on the strength of their love. We are not learning any lesson from the fact that most relationships, nowadays, have started based on *some kind of love* and they still keep failing miserably. It is amazing!

The scientific evidence about the role of human hormones in our behaviour is another proof of our misperceptions about the power of love. In particular, our hormones do not support the idea of monogamy in humans. Many studies have also shown that our infatuation and love dies within six months to two years. More details about the effects of human hormones are available in this author's other relationship books, including *The Mysteries of Life, Love, and Relationships*.

Maybe it is all right to seek love so eagerly. However, we should also remember the nature of love in general as well as the chaotic nature of relationships in the new era. We should do so to be prepared for the consequences of our futile search for love or even finding it. We should indeed concentrate on developing our Self (selflessness), instead of fooling ourselves with phony lovers or indulging ourselves with more ELove. Besides, SLove happens by accident and not active search.

Another cause for misperception in relationships is that partners use love as another yardstick for measuring equality. That is, they expect their partners to love them as much as they think (or pretend) they love their partners. They demand love-equality to ascertain the fairness of their relationships. Surely, love-equality is a symptom of the general equality fad in society. People believe that love is a spiritual feeling (Self driven), but then make it conditional on their partners' ability to love them equally. Their demands for love equality merely expose their selfishness (instead of selflessness) and destroy their chances to relax and relate more naturally.

Couples' perception and expression of love are surely not unconditional (Slove) as long as they insist on love equality. It is even more bizarre when they often retaliate harshly when they do not perceive the love they get adequate. How can this attitude have any trace of SLove in it? It is at best only a Model driven love (where partners strive to play a lover's role), without any sense of selflessness (while fussing over equality). This is just an example of partners' rising confusion everyday about their perceptions of love, which stirs more expectations from relationships. The need for equality has become such an imposing social phenomenon that it has infected even our love affairs. We are less interested in figuring out how our partners' integrity may qualify them as our soul mates. Nobody knows what the characteristics of a soul mate should be. Rather, we insist on measuring, in greatest accuracy, the equality (as well as the intensity) of the love our partners can show, which we continue to doubt, anyway.

While equality, in the sense of *fairness,* is the foundation of our democratic society, it has turned into a socio-political platform to further spread our demented social values. The term 'equality' is somewhat misused inadvertently to express our repressed anxieties, which then stirs new expectations and headaches. Sadly, the meaning and means of equality are often exaggerated, so much so it also has damaged the structure of relationships altogether. In particular, women are inclined to push for love-equality since they believe in the importance of love in relationships more eagerly than men do.

Anyway, relationships' chances of survival have declined a lot with love becoming the main success factor—as love itself cannot survive in relationships. In fact, a cynical interpretation of *love* implies that it flourishes only by deprivation and not through a relationship. Perhaps believing that marriage kills love is cynical. Yet, we can safely say that after the first stages of companionship, couples encounter a peculiar atmosphere dissimilar to their preliminary perceptions of *love*. The new atmosphere is shaped around partners' odd personal needs and personality aspects, which are hardly selfless and disciplined. Thus, in light of all these clues, both a more meaningful view of love and a better perspective of marriage are essential. The question is why cannot our culture focus on factors that are effective in prolonging relationships without depending on love too much, even and especially for starting them? The question is, 'Why cannot we identify and rely on the relevant factors of success for marriages?' The answer is that we do not realize the nature of love and relationships in the new era, yet keep raising our expectations about love. And we have not grasped the importance of building a relationship framework.

Many of us might realize eventually that our perceptions of love and ideal relationships are unrealistic, and thus lower our expectations. We may end up thinking *practical* at the end, but not before hurting our partners and ourselves a long time by letting our idealism and misperceptions raise our expectations naively. The meaning of 'practical' in this instance refers to a form of submission (resignation and disappointment), which usually prevails in relationships these days. Often we learn our lessons too late, instead of thinking practical from the start in the sense of only perceiving and working on relevant success factors in relationships. Thus, most modern marriages suffer big doses of resignation and disappointment. Then again, many good marital opportunities are lost due to our childish demands. We ruin our marriages or look for an idol until most of our useful lives are wasted on dreams. Some of us might then further damage our integrity, pride, and beliefs when we keep lowering our expectations drastically for getting into a relationship to elude loneliness, despite its obvious flaws and predictable headaches.

Obviously, the word 'love' covers many meanings and none of them really reflects true love (SLove). It is perceived and applied differently by people based on their psychological and circumstantial needs. Thus, love has no definite meaning to draw upon or use as a criterion. We can apply it arbitrarily merely to soothe our needs for compassion and companions without making too much fuss about it or expecting long-term commitment on that basis. "You said you loved me!" is a common complaint, nowadays, when couples interpret love according to their arbitrary or vague perceptions. Maybe it is time now to stop this confusion and couples' futile sufferings in their relationships.

People seek love (mostly ELove) to satisfy a large variety of their personal needs. They have some impressions about the meaning of love, and they have many motives that they try to satisfy by their expressions of love. Their main motives are:

- To *communicate* with their partners.
- To express their basic *feelings*.
- To release *psychological* pressures.
- To mimic their *spiritual* needs.
- To *control* their partners.
- To *manipulate (abuse)* their partners.

These motives drive us to use the word 'love' rather sloppily. In the absence of a better word to express our exact motives (or hiding them), using the word 'love' for so many purposes has become a norm. Yet, it is crucial to keep our expectations from exchanging 'love' phrases in a manageable perspective.

Aside from our selfish need for Elove (egotistical love), we seek love also for bringing us that ultimate happiness. We see happiness only in the arms of that special person who fits the image of a perfect soul mate. We believe we can complete our existence by finding and taming him/her. This reflects both our strong instinctual need for spiritual love (SLove) and Elove. On the other hand, our chronic ELove stirs negative feelings, such as jealousy, depression, possessiveness, and loneliness; and nothing we can usually do about this evil.

Need for Sex

Sex is a *basic* personal need, but gets complicated and touchy in relationships, nowadays. Often conflicts arise when couples' marital problems or higher needs (e.g., compassion or ELove) hinder the satisfaction of their instinctual need for sex. Sex has now become conditional upon satisfying many higher personal needs of partners, especially love and compassion that partners are often least capable of delivering. Thus, their basic sexual need is threatened when other aspects of their relationship are not perfect, which is usually the norm in modern marriages. At the same time, our zeal for sex, and our impression about its importance, has grown a lot. People have become obsessive about their sexuality and trying it with different partners.

Nevertheless, sex remains the most reasonable expectation from relationships. Since couples do not wish to look outside their relationships to fulfil this urge, they should depend on each other to satisfy this essential need. In reality, however, partners often withdraw sex as a tool for emotional blackmail or retaliation. Moreover, sometimes partners cannot cooperate in this regard, thus look for sex elsewhere. The modern social setting has spread this crooked mentality. Meanwhile, sexual freedom feels so urgent to people like a natural need with minimal ethical importance. Nonetheless, nothing can be done about this need beyond what everybody already knows and practises the best way they can. This is just another source of conflict in relationships. Other dramas surrounding sex cannot be helped, either. They are all psychologically explainable and rather inevitable.

Sex obviously has another instinctual purpose, too. The strong urge to procreate encourages especially women to seek a companion more actively. Men usually play a lesser role in pursuing this heavenly purpose (the reproductive aspect of sex, of course). Therefore, while both genders have big sexual drives, they have different motives (and biological clocks) for acting upon it. These differences lead to clashes, especially after children are born. Women focus more on the welfare of children and become too possessive of them. Sometimes, it seems absurd the way they try to protect their children even from their husbands. Accordingly, men feel abandoned and neglected both sexually and emotionally. They might also face occasional hostility when their interference or means of child rearing agitates their wives. On the other hand, men are often accused of their shallow pursuit of sex, although women are catching up in this regard, too. The need to experiment with our sexuality is now in full swing by both genders.

Anyway, nobody can be blamed for the way their sexual instincts dictate their behaviour and priorities in life, or when their lifestyles jeopardize the satisfaction of a basic need like sex. Sex has turned into a potent parameter for partners to play their games and tame each other. These are irreversible facts that cause gender quarrels and insecurities. Yet, it is crucial to acknowledge their impacts and sources, instead of denying (or arguing about) them tenaciously. Women's growing share of sexual activities and appetite, plus their progressive approach and perceived deprivation regarding sex are emerging social phenomena that would continue to change marriages' format and widen gender conflicts and quarrels.

Need for Equality

Women's urgent need for *a sense of* equality has caused huge mayhem and gender differences, too, instead of helping them, relationships, or society. Thus, the new generations should pay a big price to resolve this matter and maybe reduce the gender gap caused by our *confused drive* for equality. For one thing, our perception of, or need for, equality has hindered the urgent need for couples to learn about the principles of teamwork and humility in order to make up for all the symptoms of gender differences wreaking havoc in the new era.

In fact, eventually teamwork would be the only means to abolish the need for equality struggles. Nowadays, we try to oversimplify, maybe even abuse, the workings of relationships by pushing the concept of equality and assuming it would solve all the problems automatically. We attempted to solve women's personal problems by reducing men's level of control and intimidation. However, it appears relationship conflicts have raised dramatically the more equality has been stressed. Even worse, women's frustration has grown due to unfulfilled expectations. The more they have fantasized about, and hoped to get from, their relationships, the less they have received (again judging by divorce rates and rising family conflicts).

Often, women's expectations for equality appear vague, sounding more like whining, with devastating effects on their relationships. Some women's exaggerated demand for equality sometimes sounds more like a quest for superiority. Initially, the equality movement sounded logical for overcoming men's domination. However, now, everything appears to be turning around. That is, men feel unequal in a world where women set most standards of equality, which seem one-sided or arbitrary. They often feel intimidated by their wives' wishes and vague expectations. Many of them have adopted a passive role in their relationships due to the severity of their wives' views of equality. The problem is that 'equality bargaining' is infected by partners' Ego, nowadays.

Ironically, equality expectations often arise from partners' urge to control one another. In fact, the concept of equality is psychologically absurd and untenable, anyway. This is true, as everyone believes that his/her logic is much superior to others', including his/her criteria for defining equality. We believe that we know everything better than everybody else regardless of his or her gender. A strong tendency in most humans is to feel superior to others, not equal, although they might pretend to be fair and humble. Now, almost everybody believes in gender equality, but not intellectual equality. By default, our Egos force us feel almost perfect in terms of logic, intelligence, cognition and all the rest of the good attributes. The gender equality issue is resolved for the most part, but the inherent sense of superiority can never be erased from people's minds —due to their deep belief of their intellectual superiority. This is the source of all the inequalities, nowadays. They are not gender driven, but rather Ego driven for both genders. Gender equality is a hot issue now due to the relationships' growing importance and troubles in society, and since everybody feels special and superior and not equal.

Clearly, 'equality need' frictions can be reduced only by developing and propagating the sense of teamwork. If partners learn to focus on teamwork, their obsession for *equality would* subside. Relationships' success would be measured only by the smooth operation and outcome of teamwork—not the level partners' equality or superiority. Equality is perceived and gauged differently by people based on their subjective criteria and emotional maturity, anyway. Thus, instead of wasting so much energy on forcing some kind of imaginary equality in relationships, couples must learn to put all those efforts into defining a practical process of cooperation and harmony. Teamwork enables couples to contribute to major decisions and feel active in their relationships. Still, it does not deprive partners from doing most tasks independently based on their expertise or merely for creating synergy. Partners must be able to decide independently, instead of doubting their authority or identity all the time. They should not lose their confidence and the control of their lives in fear of retaliation.

Indeed, the strength of teamwork lies in its emphasis on partners' independence and objectivity. Their independent (yet objective) opinions are needed for important family decisions. This is more in line also with the trend in society to promote individualism. However, it gives partners a chance to use their unique expertise for their relationship's benefit without being second-guessed by their partners. In teamwork, partners' roles are apparent unlike the existing approach, where partners are confused or depressed regarding their roles, as they are mostly preoccupied by equality games. It is indeed tough to grasp the equality rules, since we have not yet established the objectives and means of *family equality*. Equality, and measuring it, are at best vague and arbitrary. It lives only in our imaginations and it manifests in the form of immature games of resistance and confrontation with no definite purpose or guideline.

The concept of 'equality' has initially emerged out of a sense of desperation, but is now being driven mostly by Ego—the urge for superiority. Teamwork, on the other hand, is Self (goodness) and Model (tactfulness) driven. Therefore, it is not too difficult to decide which approach could have a better chance of success in the long run. Couples' quarrels to exert equality would only reinforce the Egos of both partners, which would only lead to more clashes. Besides, as said before, the concept of equality is psychologically flawed, anyway, since our prominent Ego absolutely abhors equality. Most people are psychologically incapable of handling equality, because they feel superior in their deepest level of consciousness.

While genders have the same rights and acknowledge each other's contributions, they need not share the same tasks and roles to ensure equality. This is a clear concept, but in reality men and women waste a lot of energy, nowadays, consciously or subconsciously, on measuring the difficulty of their varied responsibilities and quarrelling about them.

The best test of equality in terms of partners' sharing of household affairs or decision making is to see how well those activities and processes fit within the guidelines of teamwork. If they do not fit, they are biased, Ego driven, and futile. On the other hand, understanding the guidelines of teamwork and implementing them in relationships would enhance partners' Self and Model at the expense of Ego—thus more effective relationships. In all, teamwork guidelines would automatically ensure couples' fairer treatment of each other, which is the goal of equality struggles theoretically. By adhering to some basic guidelines for relationships (and teamwork), partners' rights is best served in an environment built for coexistence. So the question is, if any teamwork standards can be invented what would they look like?

Need for Individualism

In line with our struggles for independence and equality, the notions of individualism and identity have introduced further complications in relationships. In particular, they have caused additional gender differences and major barriers for couples' appreciation of the need for teamwork and synergy. Since we insist so much on proving our identity and individualism, it is important to at least know what they mean and maybe learn to acquire those qualities truly. In fact, individualism has a lot to do with being a good person, which is the best way to improve our relationships and reach gender equality, too. Alas, we do not know how to define and develop our true individualism in a natural way.

Individualism is the nucleus of 'self,' as it must ensure our survival and progress, while fighting the evils of social living. Its goal is to strengthen our spirit, integrity, and compassion instead of becoming more ruthless or losing our resilience. Individualism portrays the simple and pure characteristics of an evolved person with a transcended soul. His/her integrity and compassion lead him/her to deal with others fairly and avoid wickedness. Most of all, individualism reflects the traits of a person in peace with him/herself and the world despite the pervasive societal imperfections and evils.

Defining 'individualism' as a transcended state of being reveals our justified mistrust in the inherent purity of human nature. It reflects our realistic view of human character and its influence on our cultures and lifestyles. It shows our desperate struggle with humans' natural tendency towards immorality as their basic qualities. On the other hand, our societies hinder the advance of individualism as a common human attribute. Sadly, individualism and integrity often sound like some rare virtues found only in saints and highly evolved individuals—like divine manifestations beyond most humans' capacity.

Humans' low integrity affects them mostly in relationships, but also personally. One becomes what he practises as part of coping with all the hypocrisies and deceit in society. Present social setting forces us to become cruel like everybody else, despite our potentials to be a better human being. We witness people who have become so absorbed in their evilness that malice has become their real nature. They cannot do anything without some treachery even when it has no direct benefit for them. Their individuality has been simply reduced to a mere deceit-brain. Strangely enough, they actually fall for their own lies with such deep commitment they often sacrifice even their valuable possessions in the process, including their families and friends. The world of hypocrisy they choose to live in a lifetime contradicts even the raw social ethics, let alone a sense of modesty. They just float within a vastly crooked illusion of life and behave like the devil.

The Webster's dictionary defines individualism merely as, 'The conception that all values, rights, and duties originate in individuals.' Thus, individualism seems like an attempt to gain our independence and identity, not just in society, but mostly in our own heads. We try to 'know (about) ourselves' and the possibility of being a better person. Thus, we strive to assess ourselves in terms of values, rights, and duties that we have adopted in the process of developing and proving our identity.

We try to understand where our values come from, how authentic they are, and how they help humanity and us. In terms of our rights, we ensure they coincide with the rights of others, so that all individuals and society as a whole can move towards harmony and relief from life's hardships. Still, the problem, nowadays, is that people or genders' rights often turn into self-serving demands on others and society for personal gains and interests. People have difficulty realizing this flaw when looking for their rights. They merely try to impose their misperceived rights on others deliberately or inadvertently by their egoism and unrelenting struggle for power and authority with little regard for the rights of other human beings.

With respect to our duties, individualism emphasizes on our personal obligations and social responsibilities. Some of them are instinctual, such as our duties towards our children and parents. Other duties, e.g., towards society and family, are expected to come natural to us, too, if genuine individualism drove us. Yet, in reality, people are too self-absorbed these days to maintain their integrity and fulfil these types of duties naturally. Therefore, they should extend extra efforts more consciously to discharge their duties to some degree at least. Some duties at work and society are mostly moral obligations rather than instinctual, of course.

Still, our passivity in acknowledging and discharging our duties may be intentional or due to mere ignorance. Intentional passivity is hard to repair, as it mostly reflects our pomposity, psychological flaws, and the impact of social adaptation. On the other hand, ignorance can be cured a bit easier through self-awareness and involvement.

Overall, individualism reflects the quality of our choices, decisions, and actions, as we determine and practise our rights, values, and duties for accomplishing notable purposes. While the objective of 'individualism' is to strengthen the inherent value of 'self' as a wise and humble person, it also stresses on personal integrity to adjust our values, rights, and duties in line with the needs of humanity. Individualism is not only an inner growth and fulfilment, but also an outer reflection of integrity and morality. The Webster's definition of 'individualism' does not quite reflect the need for the rightness of one's values, rights, duties. However, without integrity and compassion, we cannot set the right 'values,' as we cannot see their rightness.

And we cannot comprehend the value of people's 'rights,' since our criteria of rightness is personal and selfish. Contrary to the common view to interpret individualism as a means of self-absorption, its value lies mostly in humility and a person's regard for other individuals' rights. In fact, individualism is an inner exploration, instead of a phony, outwardly show of one's Ego, the way it is mostly implied in our common pretensions of individualism.

Individualism evolves gradually only through compassion and modesty, while a person gauges the truthfulness of his connection to other individuals, things, and concepts with a genuine interest and care. Only then, s/he can see the rights of other individuals and the values of things and concepts in their purest sense in line with his/her own authentic life purposes. Without compassion and integrity, one lacks the sensitivity and sensibility required for perceiving things or people outside one's rigid and biased prejudgments. The lack of compassion and modesty reflects Ego domination, which remains the main hindrance for knowing our 'self.'

Trying to teach people 'individualism' without including all the above noted basic requirements in our definition has been the cause of the present misperceptions about this divine notion. The result of our superficial grasp of individualism has been disastrous, because people interpret this concept as a means of becoming more haughty and demanding, instead of learning humility. It has caused more gender differences and relationship conundrums for people who have no capacity to go beyond the superficialities of our society, including its dire definition of individualism.

As one of the seven dimensions of 'self,' individualism is a source of energy, too. The energy stems from the integrity of our choices, decisions, and actions. A serene sense of 'self'-realization lifts our spirits when we finally choose a modest option after pondering many self-serving possibilities, make a compassionate decision, or take a worthy action. We strive to make the right choices with integrity and compassion for the betterment of humanity and for developing our own spirits, despite our sour experiences and the normal distractions of social living. Perfecting every dimension of 'self' brings more energy and wisdom for living peacefully with contentment. This proactive mentality helps us build our integrity and spirit to go through life with minimal confusion and distress.

This mentality may help us understand that, contrary to our immature perception, individualism has nothing to do with self-centredness and egoism. Rather, it is merely the means of reaching our Self and a sense of selflessness.

Need for Fairness

Equality, independence, and similar self-boosting objectives in the new era are for getting a sense of fairness and justice. We firmly believe that life owes us the best of everything. We are convinced that we not only have huge potentialities to offer to society, but also deserve substantial rewards for what we do and who we are. We strive to demonstrate our potentialities so that people can discover and respect us. We change our jobs, invent things, offer our ideas, and pursue all sorts of business ventures in order to prove ourselves.

However, many forces prevent our dreams from coming true. Most of us realize gradually that our potentialities would never be recognized or rewarded; therefore, we attribute this atrocity to the world's unfairness. It hurts a lot, but also feels as though people deliberately refuse to acknowledge us for what we do, think, say, and feel—our unique potentialities. They refuse to provide enough feedback, encouragement, rewards, or respect, which we adamantly believe we deserve. Thus, we become frustrated and convinced that both life and people are unfair. We get this feeling a lot in our relationships, especially, which then leads to lots of gender clashes and quarrels.

We often feel ignored and misunderstood. Our cynicism about life's unfairness and people's malice is often warranted, actually. Naturally, while everybody is self-centred and mostly concerned about his/her own needs, desires, and Ego, fairness becomes an illusion automatically. Our unfairness is not out of malice necessarily, but because of our self-serving attitude and a sense of being fairer and nicer to ourselves first. We need the most and best of everything for ourselves and those whose friendship and loyalty we need. If any charity is still left in us to share, only then we might be less prejudiced occasionally. These are real facts and we should accept that we cannot do anything about the matter. The rule is that most people lack enough compassion towards others, especially strangers—the primitive law of survival and success!

Another point is that we are often personally responsible for stirring the feelings of unfairness by exaggerating our needs and potentialities and setting unreasonable expectations. That is, actually, a sign of our unreasonableness (unfairness) when we expect people to appreciate 'who we are' while we keep overstating our capabilities with arrogance. Even if we were honest with our presentation of who we are, it is not usually possible for others to appreciate who we are. Thus, ultimately, either our perceived sense of unfairness or actual prejudices in society cause us stress and confusion. Still, we must somehow learn to come to terms with this sad reality, too.

Feeling unfairness and inducing it ourselves are inevitable social realities mostly due to humans' inherent shortfalls. This awareness provides a basic consolation, since we can mostly blame humans' nature for our actions and feelings. Still, some people can handle unfairness better. They disallow of self-pity or aggression overwhelm them when they face unfairness. If we do not measure our potentialities and self-worth in terms of external rewards and recognition, the feeling of unfairness hurts to us less frequently, too. In addition, when a person develops his/her inner confidence and actualizes his/her potentialities realistically, the question of unfairness hardly surfaces.

Ultimately, we have two choices on this matter. One option is to take unfairness as an irreversible reality—like so many other bizarre limitations of social living—even in our family relationships with our spouses and children. This mentality is hard to adopt, but it can save us a lot of agony and energy. More importantly, this mentality can help our relationships, too. The other more prevalent option is to let self-pity raise our distress and aggression towards others. Taking fairness less seriously helps us make wiser choices in life, however. Instead of aggression or self-pity, we could ponder the possibility of creating a life of self-reliance and independence, while hoping for the likelihood of humans becoming less self-serving and selfish eventually.

Indeed, we deserve to be understood and appreciated, but it is somewhat unreasonable to expect others to care enough, or be able, to perceive our feelings and thoughts accurately or fairly. People have too many personal problems and plans to care about other people's personality, potentialities, and ideas. Their judgments are at best hasty if not malicious. This is the rule and sentiments of the perceived world. It is human nature now, since we have not built our spirits, especially the spirit of fairness. We must accept the reality of unfairness, despite the pervasive discriminations and prejudices at work and home. As another challenge for exploring our divine potentialities, it is important to adjust our perspective of unfairness and our expectations from people. Growing this kind of mentality is difficult, especially towards our spouses, yet it is becoming a necessity to curb gender quarrels.

Need for Control

It is bizarre that we are so obsessed about fairness, equality, independence, and all other personal needs discussed in this chapter, but still are so eager to control others and their needs. We like to control everything to keep order in our lives. We strive to foresee events or obstacles that might jeopardize our welfare. The more complex our relationships and societies have become, the more we feel a need to imagine and control the sources of potential threats to our physical and mental welfare. This is particularly true nowadays, since we trust people much less, even our families, than we did a few decades ago. We know that crooks are everywhere, trying to take advantage of our naïveté. Accordingly, our defence mechanisms and need for control have grown fast to survive in this atrocious setting. Even banks, stockbrokers, real estate agents, and supposedly government-controlled entities often lure us into bad decisions and losing our life savings. Hardly do governments step in to support citizens because capitalism gives a higher priority to free enterprise than to individuals. Thus, we feel the pressure to control our lives better and ensure we are not victimized.

As we get into relationships, the need for control feels even more urgent and necessary. We must protect our families and ourselves, while we must also be careful about our families' intentions and likely hidden agendas. Sadly, the more society advances, the less we can trust our partners in relationships. Thus, we try to control them in order to minimize the chance of getting hurt by them. We also wish to control them with the assumption that it would be the best way to keep and prolong our relationships. Naturally, the result of all this controlling is that couples hate, and stress out, each other. Couples' needs for independence is challenged when partners try to control each other in hopes of making their relationship last longer. Thus, the need for control is a major cause of gender quarrels.

It is just too weird that we do not grasp the personal inner turmoil and pains that our conflicting needs for both control and independence cause collectively in society and marriages.

Even love is often abused to satisfy one's need for control. One reason for 'love' being in such demand, nowadays, is that a person can supposedly control his/her partner better if that partner remains in love with him/her. We yearn for SLove to fulfil our needs for 'self'-realization and spirituality. However, in reality, we mostly end up seeking ELove for compassion and/or controlling our partners. We crave love, even though we are often not capable of giving love in return. We want to be loved for several reasons noted in this book, but also for controlling our partners through love dependency.

Overall, our spirits and potentialities are usually dampened in relationships due to partners' urges to control each other, sometimes even through (real or fake) love. Thus, partners lose their chances for personal growth and self-actualization when even one partner is a control freak.

Need for Manipulation and Domination

If our need for control gets out of hand, we strive to manipulate or dominate others like an obsessive, sadistic mission. The evil of domination and exploitation is not as common as humans' need for control, yet it is now spreading fast like an epidemic in our haughty societies. In marital relationships, in particular, the need for domination has intensified due to the high level of emotions involved and the proximity of couples' activities and decision-making needs. It is weird when couples (especially women) insist on equality, but seem capable of attaining such presumed sense of equality only through domination. As two main contributing factors, egoism and domination taint almost all relationships. When we communicate with one another, we rush automatically to dominate (or manipulate) the situation and our partner by pushing our point and position fiercely to win at all cost. Our attempts to change our partner are again the symptom of our inner urges to dominate and turn him/her to a personality of our liking and preference. Thus, we look for excuses to blame and nag, mostly since we never feel to have enough domination and influence over others. It also reveals how some of us abhor curbing our urges and intentions of dominating our spouses and the family structure. Blaming and nagging are largely personal tactics to wear down our partners and take over the situation and decisions.

Of course, signs of teamwork and cooperation occasionally emerge mostly through Model. However, soon enough, our Ego takes over and proceeds to dominate the situation and our partner. Naturally, we all strive to conceal our obsession for domination and manipulation, especially before marriage when we use our Model to manoeuvre and soften the person we like. Then, our suffocating urge for manipulation and domination eventually erupts with full force.

Our obsession for domination of family life and our partner obviously reflects our intention to control everybody's actions and behaviours. We need to do this in order to ensure things proceed according to what we think is best for our family. We strongly believe in our good intentions to stop our marriages' demise, while controlling our fate and independence as much as possible, too. When our needs for control and independence are threatened by our spouses' objections and interferences, we feel the need to dominate them and the situation. We abhor surprises, risks, and troubles. We like everything to proceed smoothly as we have planned personally and perhaps with input from our parents or friends. We simply feel a need to run family issues and situations. However, when we find out that our spouse likes to influence those same issues and situations, we are left with no option but to control our partner as well. Thus, the logical tactic in our minds is to control any situation and person that may affect the outcome of our plans and needs for a kind of life and relationship we like. We also expect our partner to sense and agree with our values, outlook, and logic. We believe our lifestyle is the most logical one, so everybody should agree with it after we explain it to him/her, in our often crooked language. However, if we cannot come to agreement soon, we still plan and persist to remain in control somehow, or else we get agitated and retaliatory all the time.

Our urge for domination also emerges from our desires to possess our partner like a personal property. Possessiveness by itself is a psychological defect that most of us are inflicted with somewhat. It stirs our need for domination of the physical aspects of our partner's life, such as what s/he does or wears, where s/he goes, and how s/he feels and thinks. We want our partner think in certain ways for our convenience, but more so, we want to be in control by possessing him/her mind.

Surely, our urges for domination and possessiveness hurt our partner and relationship, but also degrade our individuality and peace. They stir our jealousies, retaliations, nagging and blaming, and many other destructive psychological reactions. The energy and time we waste on retaliations and confronting people with stress are enormous, while our senses of jealousy and possessiveness paralyse our brains and deprive us from pursuing rewarding and relaxing activities. Most of us grasp this fact in the latter stages of our lives when the futility of our jealousies and retaliations become clear.

Instead of drowning ourselves in a state of helplessness by our possessiveness and domination, mostly due to desperation for love and attention, we can focus on our essential personal needs. We can attend to the joint needs of partners (especially for independence and equality) in modern marriages.

Needs for Dependence and Independence

Genders' conflicting needs for independence and dependence were discussed in the previous chapters, including points 5-6 on pages 29-30 and points 9-10 on pages 36-38. The unique ways partners perceive and attend to these needs stir the most amount of gender conflicts and quarrels. Accordingly, these contentious personal needs are elaborated further here as well as the Reverences at the end of the book.

We get into relationships mostly to relieve our loneliness. However, in reality, many relationships make partners feel the ultimate sense of loneliness. The sense of physical loneliness might be remedied somewhat by living under the same roof with a partner. Yet, psychological loneliness gets even fiercer when partners fail to relate and communicate. Relationships raise our sense of loneliness many folds, because we feel the difficulty of relating to another person tangibly, and since we had imagined we could do all that rather easily, mostly on the power of love alone. Most of us had never felt so desperate and lonely psychologically when we had been living alone. We are badly disappointed after all those years of daydreaming about finding a partner to relieve our loneliness. Thus, relying on our partners to cure our psychological loneliness is simply an unreasonable expectation.

Another hurdle is that even if our partners were capable of satisfying our need for dependence, we sabotage their efforts personally by our constant expressions of individualism and independence. Our false pride stops us from expressing our need for dependence and our partner's moral support directly. Instead, we try to prove, and pretend, stubbornly to be tough and self-reliant emotionally. Showing our neediness could tilt the balance of power, after all. Meanwhile, we strive to fulfil both our dependence and independence needs just by playing some superficial roles and expecting our partners to not only grasp their meanings, but also respond favourably. Yet, these conflicting (unexpressed) expectations and knotty role-playing only frustrate both partners. Our partner recalls our previous shows of independence, especially when we suddenly play the role of a vulnerable partner seeking dependence. Showing the right balance of dependence and independence and clarifying the timing and areas we need our partners' support is difficult. We might imagine that we are doing a good job of it, but that is only another selfish assumption and gross misperception.

Our failing struggles for independence and dependence also make us jittery regularly. Thus, we react unfavourably towards our partners, unjustifiably, especially when we assume they are refusing to understand our needs intentionally. Naturally, when a partner seeks independence and finds his/her partner a hurdle in achieving it, he/she feels hurt and resentful towards his/her partner. And he/she gets frustrated as well when he/she needs attention and dependence, yet his/her partner is incapable or reluctant to provide it. The situation gets out of hand, as their relationship remains undefined in terms of partners' needs for dependency and independency. Partners' erratic attempts to be independent or dependent also confuse them, especially when they do not get the kind of responses they expect. They get sad and frustrated, yet do not realize their own difficulty or apathy to recognize and respond to their partner's incongruent needs for both independence and dependence.

These dual deprivations stir deep inner conflicts for partners already, as will be discussed in Chapter Ten. Yet, partners' inner conflicts heighten when their needs for dependence and independence do not align in terms of timing and their mood fluctuations. It hurts them deeply, since their personal (innate) needs for dependence and independence are badly imbalanced and ignored. This gross incongruity causes constant frictions between partners, while they also criticize each other's erratic needs. All along, partners' rotating struggles for more freedom or attention come across too unnatural and inconsistent. Thus, both partners believe that his/her mate is instable or neurotic. They also believe that their partners' expectations are illogical or even out of spite. Thus, instead of grasping and facing their conflicts logically, they react negatively by confrontation and retaliation, which means the whole relationship mechanisms, including communication, stop working.

Overall, handling our partners' unrealistic expectations for dependence and independence is hard, especially in the eyes of an impatient partner who is unable or unwilling to cope with such conflicting demands frequently. Ironically, people's needs for both dependence and independence are increasing simultaneously every day. As noted before, people are getting too spoiled and needy due to the effects of crude social values. They ask for more compassion (dependence), while also stress on their freedom and identity (independence). Thus, while partners accuse each other of behaving erratically, they face merely more arguments and frustrations. Instead of discussing their relationship dilemmas objectively and calmly, they focus only on dominating the situations and each other, or opt for separation. The feel obliged to either adapt to this confusing environment (passively or spitefully) or ask for a divorce. Both options are obviously torturous.

In our modern way of thinking, we accept open-mindedly that both dependence and independence are essential needs, and we naively believe we can cope with this major dilemma in our relationships. We might even assume we could align our needs for dependence and independence by some magical power perhaps. We assume we can make compromises so that partners can satisfy their rotating needs for independence and dependence by commonsense. This is just another unrealistic expectation.

So, what is the solution? Since our emphasis, nowadays, is placed on independence, **we must stick to independence and assume that modern relationships are no longer capable of satisfying our need for dependence** ***at the level desired.*** We should also prepare ourselves to deal with our inner conflicts (due to inadequate dependence) without blaming our partners. Many readers might object: 'What is the point of being in a relationship if partners cannot depend on each other totally?' This valid question is answered later, especially in Reference 7 at the end of the book. However, the bottomline is that we cannot really demand independence so strongly and yet seek dependence erratically. This does not make sense, nowadays. Analysing this complex puzzle is what this book is all about.

We might still count on our partners' integrity, cooperation, support, and teamwork, but cannot demand total dependence realistically. Couples must learn to be satisfied with a 'limited level of dependence subject to their relationships' health,' but never total dependence. We should learn to accept this reality gracefully without making too much fuss or noise about the lack of either enough dependence or independence.

Of course, **not fussing about dependence does not mean that partners do not advocate teamwork, compassion, and all the other good things that they should do together to make their relationship flourish.** Showing compassion with Model and MLove would help the health (and dependency level) of relationships when couples notice their partners' need for dependence, despite their arrogant show of independence. Staying civilized towards each other in those circumstances is a good gesture. However, when we keep switching between our independence and dependence urges and roles in relationships, we should also expect that our partners lose their sensitivity and sympathy about our needs. Meanwhile, partners' tensions grow, while they are unaware of the ongoing rivalry between their conflicting needs for independence and dependence. They sense only their partners' apathy even when they continue to play many conflicting and idiotic roles themselves, including retaliation, to draw each other's attention.

Advocating independence in relationships might also seem inconsistent with the purpose of 'enforcing teamwork.' Yet, 'teamwork' is an objective negotiation process between two independent partners, and not a sign of partners' dependence on each other.

Nonetheless, the options are clear: We could either keep looking for magical compromises, or agree on a set of sensible principles that best fits couples' mentality in modern societies. These practical principles, of course, lean towards partners' higher independence. New trends show that couples consider independence their most urgent personal need, and give it the highest priority in their marriages, too. Thus, we can say that:

"Since we humans are usually unable to handle the rotating demands of our partners for independence and dependence, we must adopt a relationship model to deal with the situation consistently. The escalating social fervour for independence suggests that, as a rule, couples should choose a relationship model that has the highest potential for guaranteeing partners' independence. Accordingly, partners should also reduce their expectations from relationships in terms of satisfying their dependence needs as well."

Whether we like it or not, it is now time to check and refine our assumptions regarding partners' conflicting needs for both dependence and independence. It is now time to get realistic and stop the pains of our useless struggles in relationships. All these facts must be clear to couples at the outset before getting married, because the idea of 'dependence' has been losing its practicality in relationships, nowadays. Then again, couples' mere awareness of this gloomy, growing weakness in modern relationships might help them think deeper and find ways of mitigating their marital conflicts by becoming both realistic and more compassionate.

Nevertheless, couples should ponder these realities and plan their relationships according to the assumption that partners' sense of independence must get the big priority in all respects regardless of the length and survival of their relationships. This mentality would, ironically, encourage smart people to learn teamwork and compromise, communicate easier effectively, exchange compassion, and build manageable and successful relationships. However, starting on the wrong foot, i.e., hoping that their needs for dependency would be totally satisfied in their relationship, is just opening the door for major conflicts and disappointments.

The relationship models (success factors) discussed in other books by this author place the highest emphasis on partners' degree of independence. In fact, our need for independence has become the locus of all other relationship expectations. Our drive for independence has affected all the expectations we had traditionally envisioned for relationships, including financial dependency or security.

As noted before, the worst case is when a partner is really craving security and dependence upon his/her spouse, but keeps playing the role of an independent person forcefully, while also nagging about his/her partner's insensitivity. We do not realize how we are restricting our partners' abilities to feel our need for dependence. We do not realize that our sudden need for attention (and expecting our spouses' quick response and automatically, too) is frustrating them, as well as us.

Further discussions about human needs for dependence and independence are included in the References at the end of the book in order to raise partners' awareness further about this essential source of gender conflicts.

In line with this book's limited and unscientific findings, a cynical hypothesis by this author might explain a few essential things regarding genders' personal needs clashing and stirring many weird relationship problems. That is, the author believes that people usually feel chemistry towards individuals whom they are not compatible with in any justifiable measure. The hypothesis stipulates also the opposite: Compatible individuals often feel little or no chemistry towards one another. Still, the latter group has a better chance of building and managing a good relationship compared with the first group, i.e., those incompatible lovers. If these theories hold water, the *wise* question is, 'Why would Nature make couples choose wrong partners for themselves?' Is this just another one of God's cute games with His supposedly privileged, intelligent creatures?!

CHAPTER EIGHT
War Tactics

To fulfil our personal needs in our marriages, we resort to weird tactics that mostly harm our relationships and us, instead of fulfilling our goals. Humans' needs for manipulation and domination are, especially, desperate tactics they use in hopes of satisfying their other needs. Some other demented tactics we use in our troubled marriages include withdrawal, retaliation, blaming, nagging, and getting emotional, as discussed below.

Retaliation and Nagging

We imagine retaliation makes our partner suffer, thus possibly goading him/her to change his/her attitude for our liking. Yet, it causes only more resistance and counter-retaliations that ruin the foundation of relationships. We also blame others and nag regularly in order to manipulate or dominate them. We do this rather naturally to relieve our general life agonies and setbacks. Thus, we grow a habit to look outwardly to blame something or somebody, instead of looking inside ourselves and detecting not only the real sources of our stress, but also how defective we are personally.

If partners trust and respect each other and have good communication skills, they might exchange compassion and sympathy, share their problems, and rid themselves of life's tensions and hardships. However, without trust and respect, partners feel spiteful towards each other. Their suggestions and ideas usually erupt in hostile tones and their marriage turns into the battleground for firing blames and nagging at each other. Having a spouse appears to be a convenient means of relieving our tensions by nagging at him/her. Yet, things get out of hand over time when partners get carried away with all these 'tension-releasing' schemes unconsciously.

Partners share many responsibilities. They make decisions and take actions that affect the whole family. Then, they blame each other for the ways joint decisions turn out, or even for outcomes that neither partner has been directly involved with or intended to do. They seek excuses to attribute a failure or problem to their partner, sometimes unconsciously, or merely in retaliation for something else s/he has done to them before. Sometimes, they are miserable because of their personal issues or failures, then find a convenient occasion to blame it on their partners somehow indirectly and generally. They might even arrive at general personal conclusions to blame their partner, for example by saying, "I've lost all my confidence because of the way you have treated me!", or "I've become old because of you!", etc. Very often one partner is suffering from his/her incomplete or boring life, then finds all sorts of reasons to nag at his/her partner and blame him/her routinely even when no specific issue to bug him/her about exists.

Ironically, if we could be unmarried again by a miracle, we would most likely be as much, and perhaps more, miserable and full of failures, and nobody would be around to blame it on or nag to. In our marriages, we just condemn our partners relentlessly and recklessly for our own self-inflicted misery. And usually we feel, express, or expect love at the same time! In fact, we still expect to be *spoiled, while* we keep blaming him/her and nagging all the time! We either whine directly for not being spoiled enough, or find something to nag about merely for irritating him/her.

Often one partner has no fulfilling activities to keep him/herself amused and happy, then keeps blaming his/her partner for not finding interesting or entertaining things to do together and not giving this issue enough thought and time. The blamed partner may believe s/he is doing a lot already, and is willing to participate in other joint activities whenever possible, too, but also has some personal interests that the blaming partner does not care for. Thus, one partner's personal interests turn into the other partner's source of envy and constant nagging. S/he hopes to make her partner give up his/her hobbies, which is drawing all his/her attention (love), thus a perceived conflict and threat. Sometimes, the whole point of our nagging seems to be merely for wearing our partner out and making him/her as miserable as we are. We just hate his/her relative peace!

Conflicts arise when one or both partners cannot separate their personal needs from relationship (joint) needs, thus set their expectations erroneously. Or, when one partner's attempts to fulfil his/her personal needs (as simple as listening to music or watching sports) make the other feel neglected and mentally insecure. Sometimes, a partner prefers to do almost everything together, whereas the other has less patience for many aspects of his/her partner's activities, or prefers to do some mental or artistic works alone. These examples show that partners have not yet discussed and agreed on a suitable relationship model for them, plus other likely causes of marital quarrels.

Partners' blaming and nagging are often either deliberate or unconscious reactions, but they exhaust partners and ruin their relationship. Ordinarily, using Model, instead of nagging, can help in expressing one's sufferings and needs in a passionate, calm, and objective manner, hoping at least for some tangible communication and perhaps sympathy. On the other hand, with nagging and blaming, we lose the chance of demonstrating our honest feelings, mainly through Model or Self, to keep the situation under control. Instead, our Egos and impatience goad us to keep nagging at, and blaming, our partner with no sign of

Model's flexibility to soothe even the basic frictions that erupt in all marriages. Surely, Self is also absent all the time nagging and blaming goes on. Overall, blaming and nagging reflect our pains and frustration due to either our failures to change or manipulate our partner, or our unrelenting needs for attention.

With blaming and nagging, we actually put our partner on notice to prepare for a battle. We just convolute and agitate our relationships without concern about causing confrontation and conflict. Accordingly, both the nagger and naggee ponder and put up their defences in preparation for a war. The nagging partner is most likely empty of Model, at least at this point, and attacks forcefully with a bruised Ego. The other partner has the options of surrendering and leaving the battlefield, igniting a bigger fight, or attempting to initiate a peace negotiation. If s/he resorts to the last option, which is often wiser, s/he draws upon his/her Model to bring his/her partner and situation under control. 'Model' can make peace offerings in a constructive package and this is one of those times when Model can prove its value. We can use Model to invoke the softer emotions of our partner if possible and we know how. Once we normalize the situation somewhat through compassion, and maybe help from our Self, we can reduce Model and focus on peace terms and means of maintaining it in the long run. We should not expect things to work out fast or permanently with one or even dozen negotiations, since nagging is a deep symptom and habit that partners do not give up easily. Still, our patient efforts for peace offer the only chance left before we lose our confidence in our partner and marriage.

In addition, we need courage and patience to distinguish constructive criticism—as part of teamwork—from blaming and nagging. Sadly, many of us have difficulty in expressing our intentions properly. Therefore, even a partner's constructive criticism might be perceived as a blatant blame and nagging if it is expressed in a wrong tone of voice. As a result, partners get into needless arguments and quarrels, instead of benefiting from each other's wisdom and insight. Drawing the fine line between blame and objective criticism might become a blur if expressed wrongly or when the recipient is psychologically resistant to any type of consultation process. Anyway, both partners should realize one fact eventually: Blaming does not help or solve any problem, therefore it does not matter how hard we condemn our partner or a situation. In the end, it just does not matter whose fault it is when a couple is unable or unwilling to communicate or resolve their problems calmly. Pointing fingers of blame to each other only damages their relationship further. Partners should, instead, define and agree on real problems and causes of frictions regardless of whose fault they are.

We should stop taking our marital problems personal, even if we believe our partner is probably more in fault than we are. Instead, only goodwill, while focusing on objective thinking and solutions might resolve our marital problems. And this can happen only through calm negotiations, not personalizing the issues and blaming each other.

From our personal experiences or by referring to the lists of gender qualities and symptoms in Part I, we may draw a basic conclusion about the possibility of one gender having a higher tendency for blaming, manipulation, retaliation, and nagging. Definite proofs are not available to the author about this matter today. Yet, it seems likely that women do it more often due to their decisiveness facing men's passivity and procrastination, their higher authority in the family being challenged by men, and their deep, historical frustration with men in general. This topic will be addressed in a future book in this series.

Logic and Emotions

We use both our logic and emotions as potent tactics to satisfy our personal needs, including the ones noted in Chapter Seven. Yet, at the end, our logic seems to fail and our emotions drain during endless relationship quarrels we get into for satisfying our seemingly legitimate needs. A big hurdle in relationships is that women face relationship issues more emotionally and intuitively, while men try to rely more on their demented sense of logic, which has already made them dogmatic, anyway. Then again, both human intuition and logic seem incapable of helping us within our complex societies, nowadays. Therefore, while gender differences stir many marital conflicts, we might bring some objectivity back into our marriages only through self-awareness and by adhering to a relationship framework.

Our intuition is useful for handling some aspects of our lives, especially for exploring our sense of spirituality and Self. However, it cannot assist us with our daily routines, especially relationships, in such a complex social setting. The same thing can be said regarding the impotency of human logic. It rarely helps us, mostly because we do not have a real sense of logic and fairness for making objective judgments.

In the final analysis, unfortunately, we should agree that human logic and intuition would never be able to explain so many phenomena and questions about the universe, Creation, humanity, our relationships, etc. Yet, we refuse to accept our ignorance and apply this awareness to stop at least judging everything and everyone so adamantly. We simply refuse to admit our mistakes, not even in those cases where our crooked actions and selfish beliefs are unexplainable even by human logic, intuition, science, or plausible theories.

Self-sabotage

As a great example about the impotency of our intuition and logic, we can study the way we usually go about choosing our partners and how some forces of evil always seem to interfere. A great majority of us gets entangled in this condition due to many emotional as well as personal needs and insecurities that overwhelm us on such occasions. Our logic and intuition lose even their basic values and we choose someone with whom we have the least level of compatibility.

Obviously, partners' compatibility partially improves their chances of communicating and relating to one another easier. Objectivity is introduced in their relationships at many levels when they share some values and have compatible mentalities. In reality, however, partners often sabotage even this primary tool for stirring objectivity. That is, not only we do not know how to measure compatibility, but also ignore the clear signs of incompatibility. For example, when we are in love or need a companion, we ignore the likely hassles of incompatibility. It seems as if some evil forces are at work to make us choose the wrong partners for ourselves for weird reasons. Sometimes, we go out of our ways to ignore compatible partners in favour of incompatible ones. Sometimes, we prefer jerks, as they seem to challenge us. Many reasons exist for this behaviour. They mostly relate to some inner and outer forces that make us jump into relationships hastily. The initial chemistry that partners feel towards each other obscures their objectivity. In addition, usually we do not get an opportunity to be too choosy. When someone shows compassion and love, we stop worrying about the outcome of gross incompatibility. This is true, especially, because the hassles of relationships are not felt until we get involved in one. Or, we often believe that the next partner and the next relationship would be different, i.e., it would be nice and manageable!

Unfortunately, the value of compatibility tests is also low, nowadays, anyway. However, our persistence and preference to ignore any clue or perception of incompatibility shows the low potency and value of our logic and the dangers of intuition vividly. Still, most couples prefer to depend mostly on their intuitions, chemistry, and vain values that society and their parents have injected into their minds regarding relationships' success factors. Sometime in the far future, people may finally find access to reliable compatibility tests to know where they stand and what kind of a relationship they may be able to build together. For now, even basic compatibility tests can help couples pinpoint at least their incompatibilities and those areas of clear potential problem.

In some group therapy sessions, divorced men and women were asked to mention their main reasons for choosing their ex-spouses. Their answers were quite informative. The typical answers were as follows:

- Mother/father figure
- Out of pity, I felt sorry for her/him
- Lifestyle change
- To have children
- To stabilize my life
- To have a home
- I loved him/her (the most popular answer)

Obviously, when the initial purpose of a relationship is not valid or solid, the chances of bringing objectivity into it would be slim. After a while, couples realize their mistakes and begin to resent their partners and themselves for being dragged into a doomed relationship incapable of satisfying their needs (which are superficial most often, anyway). Other reasons for couples choosing the wrong partners are: physical attraction, lust, age, social/family pressures, psychological dysfunction, biological clock, misperceptions, ELove, obsessions, material issues, insecurity, loneliness, or a lack of meaningful criteria to use.

CHAPTER NINE
Gender Roles

So many odd trends in relationships (including 161 points raised in the next chapter) show how fast gender differences are growing with big repercussions for marriages and societies. The way genders interpret new social values, plus the absence of sensible gender roles to goad teamwork, is causing havoc, nowadays. Gender encounters have become too impulsive and belligerent without a logical framework to guide couples. They merely try to survive in their confusing marriages, push their naive perceptions of individualism, and fulfil their conflicting needs for independence and dependence. Accordingly, some couples opt for separation with minimal martial inconvenience (mostly due to a sense of low independence); and some couples accept abuse and adultery as they fear loneliness and isolation (due to their high need for dependence and compassion).

A strong force infecting relationships without anyone's fault is that women are in a crude state of transition in terms of the progressive role they like to play in society and relationships. This 'transition' mainly refers to the process of men and women developing and enforcing their workable identities and learning their relationship roles in the new era. Yet, in reality, it refers to the long period for couples, especially women, to recognize that their present expectations from relationships are not logical and feasible. Nothing will be solved and gender quarrels would only grow unless and until both genders grasp, and apply their complementary roles and identities to satisfy relationships' unique, inherent needs in a teamwork setting.

The social changes and the women's new role seem rather necessary. However, the process is not still complete, and, even worse, it has not been smooth from the start. The means and the format of women's new role are not grasped even by the majority of women, let alone by men who are expected to not only know what the new format should look like, but also respond positively. Nobody seems to know, let alone agree, where the boundaries must be drawn in order to facilitate this transition without putting men under undue pressure this time. Women wish to be assertive and express their personal needs freely. However, implementing or enforcing this radical role smoothly has not been successful yet, simply because humans' inner forces, such as ego and dogmatism, still drive people's personalities and hinder their communication. In fact, ego and dogmatism have kept escalating due to modern ideologies and women's presumed new role!

Women's transition from submissiveness to assertiveness surely requires a long period of trials and errors to reach a workable steady state. However, the present generation has no time and patience to let the genders' historical predispositions get adjusted smoothly. Even worse, women's old wounds have not still had a chance to heal. Therefore, a special situation has emerged: Women find it necessary to become aggressive in order to display the assertiveness they need urgently. Especially for many women, who do not quite grasp the meaning and mode of practising assertiveness, the only practical approach seems to be retaliation and by resorting to aggression to make their points clear. For men, though, the new demands are both confusing and threatening their identities (again considering the power of inner forces ruling their minds). Women's radical expectation from men—to overcome the psychological forces that shape their (men's) identity—is also unrealistic. They are ignoring the fact that men cannot readily revamp those inner forces built within them. Making the required changes is an extremely hard task, even in a timelier manner, even if men could agree with the changes women are expecting of them. However, women cannot wait for history to take its course. They cannot struggle forever to prove their points rationally to stubborn men. So, they must put their feet down to get things done; what other option do they have? After all, they live only one short life! They cannot wait for decades and centuries for men to learn and acknowledge the validity of the new roles for both genders. Women are tired of waiting for a miracle to make men realize the new gender roles in relationships. They must take this vital matter in their own capable hands at the cost of frustrating and alienating men. Alas, problems keep rising since neither gender knows what their roles and identities should be.

Within this confusing situation, both genders' destructive aggressions are complicating the transition process. Instead of progress, we witness sabotages and retaliation, more games, more divorces, more passivity, and family murder suicides. The bottomline is that men have lost their identities (whatever it was, good or bad) and do not understand the sensibility of what is expected of them. Women are frustrated, too, because they cannot enforce their new identity, which they believe they know what it is—an identity they believe they deserve. To women, it appears that men are resisting or careless at best. Thus, everybody is drowning in despair during this transition process. We can only hope that we eventually emerge out of this chaotic situation with new workable identities for genders. It might be only a dream, though, since nobody even knows what those identities should look like. We do not even know how the transition process may evolve without too much pain and more divorces. We have not even clarified genders' roles and needs or the format of their interactions in that supposedly innovative setting. The only plausible fact is that change, if possible at all, cannot happen overnight, especially when no one knows how this transition and the affirmation of the new roles must happen. The result of the current confusion is that both genders finally get fed up with their struggles to convince the other regarding their self-conceived new roles within some imaginary relationship rules. Accordingly, men and women are conditioned, and learn, to mistrust the opposite gender much more than their own.

Therefore, partners try to dominate one another or resort to divorce. Some might just give up and play only a passive role. Meanwhile, most couples feel trapped and their relationships remain in limbo; a bunch of men and women without clear identities, put under relentless pressure by both inner and outer forces. In this hostile marital setting, we have actually become another destructive *outer force* for our partners. And we are facing a global identity crisis as well. With no clear gender identities in our modern societies, we have been importing our vague values to less modernized nations as well! We have now succeeded in disseminating our demented ideologies to all corners of the globe and confusing the whole humanity.

Like most creatures, we humans prefer our autonomy and sense of adventure, especially sexuality, instinctually. Let us stop pretending otherwise. Our Egos (and our obsession for independence) prevent us from being dependable instinctually. The discussions in this book provide a reasonable picture of the way gender differences in fact goad men and women to resist (or even fight off) each other. Of course, this does not mean that they do not fall in love or try to support each other. However, many of these compassionate gestures are tentative or the residues of old cultural norms and religions. Nowadays, humans have to make special efforts to get along and share their lives, especially the opposite sexes.

A clear clue that humans are not instinctually programmed to live together permanently, without some form of binding principles, is their amazing craving for sexual freedom. The drive to experience sex with many partners is in most humans.

We emphasize on sex with different partners a lot, somewhat instinctually and partly as a means of finding happiness.

A cute, corny *relationship* instinct is that men usually try to avoid commitment, while women want to lure them into a lasting relationship. Is this merely a symptom of the women's innate need for procreation? Probably not, as women and men of all ages have these contrary urges. Are men's avoidance and women's temptations only a 'condition' developed because of people's marital experiences throughout human history? It is hard to say, except for the fact that women seek dependency more naturally than men do, especially during maternity. On the other hand, both genders' growing resistance, nowadays, towards commitment would most likely become even more prevalent in the future as men find it more difficult every day to respond to, or bear, women's newer needs and demands and women find men less and less tolerable. With mistrust rising so fast, the future of relationships seems doomed.

We have accepted the theory of evolution that connects humans to primates and other creatures in general. In the great kingdom of God, the primary role of the male and the female is to reproduce (sexual urge). Their secondary role is to protect one another against adversaries and harsh environments. In particular, the role of the female in protecting and upbringing their offspring is quite prominent. Males are less attached to the offspring usually, and even towards the female, once the initial mating process is complete. Often the female plays a major role in cooling off the relationship, too, especially after the offspring is strong. The male obeys by keeping its distance or moving away altogether. Humans are seemingly driven by similar instincts, in spite of the social ethics devised to keep them focused, responsible, and tactful. The evidence regarding the existence of similar instincts in humans is not hard to find. We know that:

- Women are more eager to procreate. Their biological clock goads them to get this matter resolved as soon as possible. Women also have a higher urge for parenthood. Thus, they are more anxious to find a suitable man and lure him in for the ultimate goal of creating children. Although the women's inherent need for reproduction seems to compete with their rising career ambitions, this condition is mostly superficial, as explained below. Deep down, they are more attached to, and protective of, their children than men are. Actually, their need for reproduction is usually more vital to them than their urge for independence or career, unlike men. Meanwhile, women's higher urge and urgency for procreation stir their higher need for dependency on men during maternity at least.
- Women show less interest in their husbands when children begin to fulfil their emotional needs. Often, children become more important to them than their husbands have ever been. Accordingly, their urge and courage for independence grow when the main objective of nature (reproduction) is fulfilled. Of course, if husbands happen to lose their interest or their focus during this confusing process (game), women look for another mate eventually to satisfy their inherent dependency needs and passion.
- Both genders, particularly men, are lured by other people's charm once their initial attraction to their spouses wears off. Especially when people age, they crave the company of younger people. They feel vibrant and young when they get the attention of the opposite sex and often believe they can revive their youth by pursuing new adventures, instead of continuing the same boring life routines with an old, nagging spouse. All of us have this weakness—perhaps a natural way of responding to our psychological need for adventure and fear of aging. The fact that some people do not act upon this natural feeling, due to their sense of ethics, fear, or integrity, does not change the primary principle about people's natural urge to experience love and sex with someone else other

than their spouses. If we get the opportunity, only seldom we resist the temptation.

- People resent monotony and get depressed if new adventures are not instilled in their lives rather regularly. Living with the same partner often becomes too monotonous.
- The evidence about human hormones indicates that we are not content to live with a partner and in fact have an urge to satisfy a variety of our emotional needs with many partners.

Therefore, people are not mentally (or instinctually) built to tolerate monogamy for many years, especially in a society like ours, which gives so much value to pleasure and making the best use of our lives.

The Prospect of Gender Differences

The risks of the rising gender alienation due to all the points made in this book need deeper scrutiny by both the public and governments. The increasing level of relationship conundrums would affect societies immensely in the coming years in at least four ways:

Marital Relationships: The state of marital relationships will continue to deteriorate as couples feel more alienated and do not understand the roles they should play as a spouse. More relationships would also fail when couples do not understand their gender identities and cannot find means of relating and communicating effectively without too much friction.

Personal Turmoil: People's mental and physical health is threatened significantly, as they fail to find good companions, managing their relationships feels cumbersome and painful, or face the hassles of separation and raising their children alone.

Children's Mindsets: Family alienations, because of gender differences and incoherent gender identities have weakened not only family values and structure, but also couples' abilities to teach the right stuff of life to their children. Instead, children are spoiled and misled regarding life's purposes and capacities. Accordingly, their frustration and confusion about life would keep growing and leading to psychological malfunctions and self-destruction, while hurting their families and societies as well.

Next Generations: As alienation and gender differences rise, and while children are not getting the right education about life, every generation would face more turmoil, self-alienation, relationship failures, and depression.

CHAPTER TEN
Gender Encounters

Genders' genetic differences and peculiar attitudes cause so much marital conflicts as discussed in Parts I and II. This chapter reviews the effects of new social trends on widening gender differences. It also offers a comprehensive list of the major sources of gender quarrels. Accordingly, the debilitating effects of these trends, especially couples' idiotic expectations from their partners, highlight the doom future of humanity and families. Couples' awareness of the nature and effects of gender conflicts might help them modify their mentalities somewhat to create better means of teamwork and relating.

We are living in a new era satiated with many superficial needs and ideologies by conceited, ambitious people who are too obsessed with finding love and happiness, but have little patience and compassion themselves. While genetics plays a role in gender differences, many outer forces in society deeply affect couples' mentalities and behaviours in their relationships as well, which then heighten gender differences rapidly and imprudently. In fact, the rising couples' conflicts and quarrels can be attributed mostly to the effects of social disorder, since genetics could have not changed this fast over a few decades. Nevertheless, the new social trends are setting the foundation for gender encounters and quarrels more than ever in history.

Rise and Results of Gender Conflicts

More shocking than the effects of fast changes in social setting and couples' rising inability to relate is the accelerating gender differences and quarrels in the new era due to the following relationship facts:*

The Bottomline

1. Our economic systems, mainly consumerism, are deforming our social values and mentalities. People have gained a big appetite for pleasure, wealth, and crude ideologies even at the cost of ruining their marriages, all in the hopes of finding more love and happiness.
2. Consequently, the basic needs of relationships are ignored in the mass of superficial values, misperceptions, and naive slogans. 'Life is too short' and 'you live only once' have become the main mottos for most of us, especially women. Therefore, people jump out of their relationships to find a better partner to enjoy their presumed short lives the best they can. Women are more active on this matter (asking for separation), too—around 70% of all cases.
3. The rise in personal needs (for objects and compassion) has directly resulted in the decline of both moral and morale in society, while couples have raised their expectations from relationships enormously, too.
4. The impact of unrealistic expectations from relationships has been two folds: First, it has created an additional sense of deprivation and personal stress that infects relationships. Second, we now believe that relationships can fulfil many of our emotional and financial needs. Couples assume that their partners are psychologically capable of providing the love they seek. They demand more attention and affection

---

*Readers are encouraged to apply the gender quirks discussed in Part II of this book, e.g., about women's higher aptitude for Model and love, to all the points raised in this chapter and draw their own conclusions, too, about the rise of gender differences and quarrels.

to soothe their personal hurts and the stress of living in our chaotic societies. Thus, in effect, couples are weakening the potency of their relationships, which in turn increase their personal pains and anxiety.

5. Couples try to live beyond their means at a higher standard of living they afford or often deserve. They demand more regardless of their means and the added mental pressure, all in hopes of finding that elusive happiness. Family debt per capita in relation to their income is at its highest level ever, due to crooked family values and consumerism. The social and family crises are getting out of hand due to people's low sensibility about budgeting and their finances.
6. New societies have advocated the concepts of equality and individualism relentlessly. Partners' drive for independence and identity has turned relationships into a battleground for establishing their territory and superiority. Thus, teamwork in relationships is not gaining the needed attention.
7. Women, in particular, are more adamant to establish their equality and individualism after years of men's exploitation. Thus, gender quarrels during this transition period will rise with no prospect for a viable compromise in a century or so.
8. We now put our personal needs before relationship needs. We leave our relationships more often by the slightest signs of inconvenience or for an opportunity to find happiness in another relationship as soon as possible. Again, women seem to be more active in this front as well.
9. The traditional principles that guided relationships in the past have been abolished and now no new principles exist to direct couples anymore. No standards exist for couples to measure the health of their relationships by. Thus, they depend on their own subjective viewpoints or the advice of friends and family to justify their crooked conclusions about the state of their relationships.
10. Couples consider ‘love’ the main factor for relationship success, not only for starting one, but also for sustaining it.

The problem with this mentality has been discussed in Chapter Seven.

11. Relationships have become too complex and demanding. Couples are unaware of, i) the relationship needs, ii) how deeply they are affected by their family genes and rearing conditions, and, iii) the psychological impacts of partners' ongoing arguments. Furthermore, they forget that people's mindsets or personalities cannot be changed just because their partners are expecting them to change.
12. The number of divorces and separation has skyrocketed in the new era in line with the emerging social trends without raising adequate alarm or awareness in society. At this time, it has passed 50% mark and is approaching 60%. The point is that divorce has now become a routine feature of relationships.
13. The amount of frustration and stress in surviving marriages is rising, too, due to partners' oversensitivity and unfulfilled expectations from relationships. Partners are also burdened by their indecision about staying in or abandoning their dysfunctional relationships.
14. Meanwhile, stress levels in society and organizations have also risen drastically due to social and family complexities, work challenges, job insecurities, rising global competition, discriminations, migrations, and the authorities' obsession to only serve themselves, instead of fulfilling their social responsibilities.
15. Accordingly, the level of stress in families has increased, because, nowadays, usually both partners work outside the house and are exposed to extreme pressures, especially women, who have been subject to more discrimination and abuse in organizations.
16. All the crooked values and habits of organizations, such as power struggle, hypocrisy, and arrogance have infected family relationships, too. Partners follow the same rules to assert themselves at work and at home. Some women

might actually perceive their husbands as abusive bosses in the work environment as well as at home.

17. Personal stress due to social and relationships' demands makes couples testy and impatient as well. They bug each other exactly at the time that life is confusing enough and out of control already. And they expect each other to be more romantic, too!
18. To remedy relationship issues and boost communication, counsellors encourage role-playing and love expressions. Yet, relationship problems keep rising, which shows the impotency of existing schemes, especially role-playing. Of course, unless partners are naturally convinced about the feelings or words they exchange, their relationship's health would only worsen. Instead, all the role-playings, as well as phony social values, have made couples lose their identities and authenticities.
19. Companionship is probably the most important (basic) need of people, nowadays, but most often left unfulfilled. The importance of 'a companion' is evident in the wide range of personal needs it can potentially satisfy. Most people think and dream about a good companion, consciously and subconsciously, as much as they ponder food—as a kind of need urgency.
20. An important fact that couples ignore when they start their relationships is that, **the chances of relationships failing are higher than surviving, nowadays.** The idea of finding a soul mate usually turns into a sour fate when they only end up in substandard relationships. Couples miss this vital fact at the outset and do not do enough soul-searching and planning in advance.
21. Couples are not trained and prepared to handle either the new relationship needs, or the most likely scenario in their relationships, i.e., separation.

The Emerging Trends

The above main sources of gender conflicts along with general discussions in this book depict the reality of relationships in the new era. Accordingly, the effects of the emerging trends on relationships are reviewed in more detail in this section. Gender differences are playing a major role in the social havoc noted below and the new environment is itself creating more gender differences. These examples show the complexity and depth of relationship conundrums. They reflect that reversing the deteriorating situation of relationships would be an uphill struggle and quite time-consuming. Especially, it is crucial to grasp the bases for gender quarrels as analysed in some detail in this chapter. Understanding these trends might help couples' awareness about the nature and capacity of relationships in the new era. **References like 'people', 'men', 'women,' or 'we' do not mean everybody, but rather a significant portion of that particular category.**

22. People seem to be living in a fantasy world with substantial needs and dreams. Their ambitions and needs for objects do not necessarily match their talents and efforts, and their needs for affection do not match their capacity to exchange compassion. Even when they get wealth and compassion, they abuse it, since they are not mentally prepared to handle them responsibly. The more their selfish needs are satisfied, the haughtier and greedier they become. Still, everybody believes he/she deserves more love and things.
23. Accordingly, couples' rising superficial needs, including unrealistic expectations from relationships, have crippled the social structure to provide public services and maintain a healthy environment, which in return ruin relationships.
24. The growing unfulfilled expectations in relationships have also raised frustration, retaliation, and hostility in families and society. Partners' oversensitivity due to their untamed expectations hinders even their basic communications. For

example, we hear often these days, especially from women, a phrase such as, "He/she does not know how to spoil me!" Many relationships collapse due to this odd expectation. They do not even mind saying it so bluntly, as if 'spoiling' is a valid demand for relationships, nowadays. Especially, after many years of exploitation by men, now women want to be spoiled as though making up for the past generations' deprivations. They seek ELove, attention, and sometimes obedience, too.

25. The level of misperceptions and miscommunications have accelerated in relationships, too, and created more havoc.
26. Couples have lost their objectivity about the purposes and potentials of relationships due to their growing sensitivity, idealism, and expectations from relationships.
27. Accordingly, couples continue to leave their relationships faster, as they believe they can find another partner to fulfil their demands better and give them the love they deserve.
28. Therefore, most of us struggle a lifetime in search of ideal mates, while only a few of us might eventually realize our naivety after repeated failures.
29. Both single and married people envy each other's lifestyle, while they all miss the advantages of both lifestyles!
30. Unmarried people look for an ideal partner obsessively to complete their social identity, while they brag about their freedom as a single person.
31. And married people lose interest in their relationships fast, due to their misperceptions about a single (independent) life and the possibility of finding a more appropriate mate.
32. Besides our pleasure seeking mentality in the new era, our erratic urges for both dependence and independence are obviously playing a role in creating many misperceptions about relationships, too.
33. We have turned into a special (spoiled) generation—asking for more love, while becoming haughtier at the same time.

We do not realize that with more arrogance, we keep losing our capacity to give and receive love.

34. Children are getting even more spoiled in terms of idealism with little sense of life's realities and hardships. Thus, the deteriorating trends in relationships would go downhill for many more decades or centuries.
35. Couples judge their relationships' health arbitrarily or based on phony values, since no authentic yardsticks are available for setting practical standards and measuring the success of relationships.
36. Accordingly, couples keep insisting on love and objects as main requirements for their relationships' success.
37. Couples have little patience and interest to study the basic problems of relationships in a serious manner, e.g., reading books about practical marital facts. At best, they have only time and patience for testing some likely quick fixes, which have no ultimate value, anyway. People read those kinds of books or follow a few of counsellors' advices to show they tried to improve their relationships and still it did not work.
38. The rising gender rivalry and clashes look like some kind of war. The level of belittling, retaliations, intimidations, abuse, insults, manipulation, badmouthing, power struggles, screaming, crying, making a scene, nagging, blackmailing, and playing games just keep growing.
39. Men and women are becoming increasingly alienated due to the changing social values and couples' drive to establish their gender identities better (often at the cost of weakening the other gender's identity). As noted in previous chapters, some inherent gender differences are also adding fuel to the matter of couples' alienation in relationships.
40. Many of gender clashes are due to women's raw instinctual tendency challenging men's crude logical predisposition.
41. In reality, however, both our instincts and logic are usually flawed, anyway. Thus, often, nobody is right due to his/her erroneous perceptions and lack of objectivity.

42. Then conflicts grow, since men and women want to change each other's decision processes, i.e., to make them more logical or intuitive—more like themselves. They fail, since women's innate urges and men's logical tendencies are too deep to change quickly even if they realized the need for it. Their rooted mindsets often hinder this change to happen.
43. All along, mistrust among partners keeps rising, as marital conflicts and failures grow. While the statistics show how gloomy the situation has become, people still ask for more love to validate their relationships and find happiness.
44. Love in the absence of trust! How could couples be sincere about their love expressions when their senses of mistrust about people, including their partners, linger deep down in their subconscious? In fact, people's continued persistence on love, while their trust in it is fading fast, is a big irony, like another sign of humans' logic deficiency and their urge for the denial of reality to live in their fantasy worlds.
45. It is difficult to believe that 'trust' can be rebuilt between genders as a general social attitude in the near future and couples become truly convinced about it.
46. Therefore, while couples pretend to start their relationships based on trust, deep down they remain justifiably sceptical about it. This is true despite their convincing expressions of love and the roles they play mostly through MLove.
47. Overall, it is naïve to depend on 'love' or 'trust' to build a relationship. Instead, couples need objective mechanisms and a relationship framework to map their joint life.
48. The meanings of love, lust, and trust have been mixed and convoluted. This is causing additional mistrust and shakier social ethics. All those casual sex with many partners, while seeking love, are not congruent values or plans. Satisfying our sexual urge is a practical choice in modern society, but mixing it (up) with love is hypocritical and impractical.
49. The inner conflict due to less trust and more demand for love is felt deeper by men. This is because men supposedly

have a bit higher logical tendencies than women who are more emotional based on this book's discussions. With their lower MLove and Model, men are already handicapped in expressing love, but when trust is gone, showing love gets even more awkward for them. Women are more capable of expressing love, even when their trust is not high. This is due to their higher MLove and Model, of course. Men lack this flexibility, but women have difficulty grasping this fact, and instead wonder why men are so passive most often.

50. The general level of trust in relationships, and reliance on our partners' words, will decline in line with the upward trend in relationship failures. Thus, expressing sincere love will become even harder, especially for men.
51. Accordingly, men usually give up the possibility of finding a soul mate sooner than women do. They might look for a companion, nonetheless, but not with the aim of finding love. They seek a companion mostly out of loneliness and for satisfying their basic needs. Women remain romantic and optimistic about finding a soul mate due to their higher intuitiveness and Model.
52. In fact, women appear to have a higher need and talent for all three levels of love, i.e., ELove, MLove, and SLove than men. This aptitude pushes them to pursue love at any cost, but also get depressed deeper than men for failing.
53. Couples are unaware of their personal flaws behind their clashes, nor do they realize how badly they get damaged psychologically during their relationship experiences. They trust not only their own perfection, but also the existence of enough perfect people around to pick for companionship. Therefore, they keep searching for some untenable ideal life matching their fantasies.
54. In the older times, couples used to believe that marriage's most important goal was to share life's hardships together. They knew how difficult life really is. They were trained and willing to make personal sacrifices and help each other

sincerely. They merely played their angelic roles, somewhat intuitively, to reduce each other's burdens.

55. However, nowadays, many couples do the opposite. For one thing, people are pushing themselves to stay positive and believe that life is (or at least meant to be) splendid and manageable. Therefore, instead of sharing life's hardships, they cause more burdens for each other with a slight sign of inconvenience. Their childish expectations and dreams about happiness make them perceive any small nuisance an unacceptable barrier in their lives. Therefore, they rush to abandon their partners for the greener pastures. Today's marital goals are mainly revolving around partners' fixation for love, sexuality, and happiness.

56. Women have a harder time in satisfying their conflicting needs for dependence and independence than men do. This is due to women's growing emphasis on independence as a means of establishing their identity. This added pressure aggravates their already conflicting (innate) urges for both dependence and independence.

57. Instinctually, women seek security and dependence more than men do. Then, the more independence they build, the more dependence they also crave subconsciously. This is partly due to their craze for independence hindering the usual fulfilment of their need for dependence. For example, women are more enthusiastic to find love and a companion, since they are more optimistic about the chance of finding their soul mates, but also crave passion and intimacy deeper instinctually—due to higher need for adaptation (Model), reproduction urge, and socializing craze.

58. On the one hand, women like to rely on men for procreation and for fulfilling their higher social needs with their higher Model. On the other hand, their sense of urgency to prove their equality and independence is alienating men further. This big dilemma is raising women's inner conflict and confusion and widening the gender gap. They often do not

accept or feel this inner conflict, but most likely struggle with it subconsciously.

59. Seeking more independence is also a matter of 'life phase' for women. They feel empowered and independent due to their maternal power, while raising and enjoying their kids, but also because they presume their men are sticking around for emergencies, anyway. Once their kids are grown up and gone, though, their need for dependence takes precedence again, especially if men have strayed.
60. Intrinsically, women need high dependence on men also for support and completing their social identity, though they might not wish to show or accept this fact.
61. Men's conflict regarding dependence/independence is rather straightforward and simple. While they seek independence instinctually, they need to depend on women to fulfil some of their basic needs, including compassion and sex. They appear helpless without women, while inherently they keep valuing their own independence highly.
62. Nonetheless, both genders strive for both independence and dependence regularly, though for entirely different reasons. They go through these dependency cycles more forcefully at some stages of their relationships. They look for a mate to satisfy their need for dependence (mostly including their basic needs, e.g., sex and ELove). Soon, however, they take their relationship for granted and press for a complex need like independence (according to their crude views of independence.)
63. There is a race in society to behave pompously, strive for a lot of things and compassion, and be fiercely competitive. Everybody also likes to be highly sociable, pretentious, and popular. When people go to work on Mondays, they keep asking one another what they did on the weekend, as if gauging a person's worth and completeness.
64. Humans' inner conflicts are responsible for their confusion, stress, and suffering in life, which affect their relationships

eventually, too. Overall, humans' *elementary* inner forces to be good are always in conflict with the external forces goading them to be bad. The modern society advocates greed, hypocrisy, dominance, and arrogance just to name a few of the crooked trends in the new era.

65. People have become quite calculating and opportunistic (users), due to their negative experiences and conditioning, including their beliefs about life being short and precious. They use various schemes to boost their positions and get ahead, and they associate with people who appear useful to them in some ways. This general sense (regarding people's hypocrisy, calculating nature, and pettiness) has also tainted relationships, since partners judge each other based on their shallow criteria of life, but also their overall mistrust.
66. How can people be romantic when most of them are only trying to be practical (mostly by being so calculating and materialistic) in such a chaotic environment? These goals are contradictory. Our social setting is destroying people's perceptions of one another and 'love'.
67. Couples are becoming less capable, nowadays, to perceive and judge their relationships in its totality. They are easily influenced by their own need urgencies, and they are easily irritated by single events. The basic merits of relationships are largely ignored due to our hasty, egotistical judgments based on emotional episodes and erroneous perceptions.
68. A 'typical woman' image is developing nowadays, mostly due to women's efforts to achieve individualism, equality, and independence. They have created and portray a special role and identity for themselves. On the other hand, men have not yet tried to create and propagate an identity for themselves. They have not been proactive in projecting a picture of a typical man.
69. Still, men are stereotyped as selfish and unromantic, while, in fact, men are simply lost and without identity, because they have difficulty grasping and coping with women's

new demands. Men have difficulty defining and asserting themselves at this time, which then leads to more aggression or withdrawal.

70. Women are emotionally stronger by nature, and also due to their higher social adaptability and Model. This helps them in terms of rebounding quickly after separation. Then, the support they receive from other women helps them recover even faster and better. However, the same need for social adaptability and Model makes them quite anxious to find a new companion as soon as possible.
71. Women have been able to bond and support one another to impose the rules of relationships. They are creating a new culture that might eventually prove quite dysfunctional for maintaining relationships.
72. An advantage of women's bonding is that they get plenty of support when they leave their relationships. On the other hand, because of this bonding, and in line with the women's general attempt to propagate the new culture, they goad one another to be least tolerant of their relationship flaws and abandon their husbands quickly.
73. Thus, while women support each other better after marital separations, they might also be screwing up each other and causing premature separations, *even intentionally maybe,* by provoking one another with their progressive attitude.
74. Conversely, men do not have enough sense of empathy or Model to soothe each other's hurts once they leave their wives. Part of this deficiency relates to men's tendency to keep their emotions private to protect their pride. Women show their emotions but move on faster.
75. Women's intuitiveness, higher Model, and bonding ability also give them more resilience and optimism about life and love, which help them adapt better to disappointments and changes. Overall, they do not get too discouraged by their failures in past relationships. Yet the number of women on anti-depressants is twice that of men.

76. Conversely, it usually takes longer for men to heal their wounds and recommit themselves to another relationship, due to their lesser resilience and the lack of support after separation. This added agony teaches them better lessons. Thus, they usually delay getting into serious relationships.
77. Due to their pessimism about finding a soul mate, men are becoming passive and this is making women frustrated and more assertive.
78. Men's logic and mistrust override their emotional needs, unlike women. Yet, their lower social adaptability makes them more vulnerable in terms of submitting to women's whims out of loneliness—but not necessarily out of love.
79. Women are more social instinctually than men are, but this tendency is growing faster in the modern world. They seek a companion to fit and feel better in social gatherings, to complete their identity, and for support. Thus, they do not seek men necessarily out of love, loneliness, or for having a companion. They already have many companions in other women. Satisfying their social and security needs often takes precedence even over their craving for love.
80. Conversely, men prefer some seclusion and privacy. Thus, their need for a companion is more for avoiding the agony of loneliness, which is growing fast, too, nowadays. Men like socializing too, of course, but that is not their main motivation for finding a companion. Besides their basic urge to stir variety in their lives, men's socializing motives are mainly for complying with family values and making their wives happy, to be perceived as a sociable person.
81. Despite women's urge for a companion, and their obsession to enjoy life at its fullest, the welfare of their children often gets a higher priority. Many women postpone their serious relationships, after a marriage breakdown, until they feel their children's relative independence or readiness. Thus, considering the sacrifice they make for their children, they

believe they deserve their children's higher love, which they usually receive more than fathers do.

82. Fathers' traditional authority and respect has diminished in families for several reasons. **First,** women have assumed the ultimate role and responsibility for raising children and they perform this difficult task with absolute decisiveness and power. Children find their mothers in charge and their fathers passive with much less authority around the family. **Second,** mothers dedicate themselves to their kids, who in turn take a mental note of their mothers' devotion. Children feel a high bond with their mothers instinctually, too, the same way mothers feel towards their children. **Third,** kids see their mothers more vulnerable and needy for attention, especially because women can show their vulnerability through Model cleverly. Therefore, children feel obliged to take care of their mothers more than they see a need to sympathize with their fathers.

83. The bottomline is that men feel less involved with their kids and not getting adequate love and respect. Their wives treat them a lot like another one of the children, including the use of an authoritative tone in their conversations with their husbands.

84. Nonetheless, fathers' lower level of respect and power has made a negative impact on the health of the whole family.

85. The general trends reiterated in this book show that women have rather succeeded in creating and expressing their new strong identity after many decades of oppression by men. They have learned to be assertive and support one another to establish their individuality and identity. Conversely, men have lost theirs due to the ambiguity of the gender roles and new relationship expectations. This is an accurate picture overall, yet the ultimate outcome is questionable for both genders, but more so for societies overall. For one thing, women's success to enforce their identity depends a lot on men's reaction to their demands and the roles that

women want them to play. More importantly, both men and women can truly attain, and feel comfortable with, their identities only if they have a good companion.

86. In fact, our endless, inherent urge to find our soul mates is the best indication of our sense of incompleteness (lack of full identity) without a reliable companion. Our need for a companion is an urgent, important need. It can potentially satisfy many personal needs of humans stretching from the basic need for sex to the spiritual need for SLove. When these needs are not satisfied, only few humans might attain enough psychological security to affirm their basic gender identities in the new era.

87. Women may pretend that they understand, and are happy with, their emerging identity. However, when they reflect on their lives, they notice that their new identity is flawed and hurtful without a companion. Indeed, nowadays, they need a *competent* man in their lives more than ever now; more than men need a woman for social adaptation. This is due to women's higher Model and zeal for social activity.

88. Therefore, women's identity is questionable without a man or while they are not happy with their companion. For one thing, they would remain preoccupied and busy with the task of finding their soul mates, since they are optimistic about finding ideal partners. As stated before, men are not so optimistic about finding a soul mate, and they are less obsessed about having a companion (or even a definite identity) due to their lower Model.

89. Thus, if women's drive for identity reduces their chances of finding or keeping *competent* men in their lives, they would never find a practical identity. No matter how much resilience and assertiveness they strive to demonstrate in a presumably strong personality, deep down they feel a big vacuum. 'Competent' refers to men who supposedly have a strong character (identity). No woman would enjoy or care for a man with a weak character. A man without a strong

identity is worthless even for women. Yet, many women do not mind weakening their husbands' spirits.

90. Overall, it seems that many women prefer, nowadays, to intimidate and control their spouses than respect them. Men have had the same mentality throughout the history, too, but now women feel obliged to do the same thing, despite their slogans for equality and mutual respect in the new era.
91. Accordingly, both genders are getting more entangled with ongoing power struggles, since they find intimidation and manipulation the only option to manage their relationships.
92. It is absurd that all these conflicting forces are somehow corrupting relationship settings. Men are confused and lost for now, anyway. Yet, their innate resistance and passivity are damaging women's attempt to assert their own identity. This is especially true when the outcome is women's lesser access to *competent* men to support them mentally and physically.
93. Having emphasized enough on both genders' innate need for a companion to find their identities, a more disturbing fact is that even when they are in a relationship, neither gender can find its identity because of all their clashes.
94. Thus, genders' attempts to find their identities fail whether they are in a relationship or not, unless they adopt a more practical relationship framework to relate more effectively in line with sensible identities. The reason is that as long as the parameters for developing their identities are not pure and unselfish, partners will only keep fighting to enforce their perceptions of ideal identities for their genders.
95. In all, partners' misperceptions of themselves and their partners, plus their erroneous impressions of ideal identities for their genders, prevent them from finding their true and practical identities. Besides, their continuous clashes suck the energy out of them to find and exert their identities.
96. A cynical observation about relationships in the new era is that sometimes women seek men mostly to test and exert

their power over them; to prove their superiority and new identity.

97. Two types of role-playing are introduced in relationships, both with adverse effects. First, the role-playing schemes that marriage counsellors advocate to stir communication and love in relationships. This technique is weak as long as partners do not grasp relationships' innate problems, so playing roles only frustrates them further. These superficial communications, in fact, confuse them further, instead of making them learn about the unique relationship issues and realities, nowadays. Instead of role-playing, partners should grasp and tackle the main sources of their problems directly.

The second type of role-playing begins from the minute partners meet and continues throughout their relationship. They play all kinds of roles and games to impress, entice, manipulate, or deceive each other. They keep exaggerating in all respects to succeed: by flattering, getting emotional, showing apathy, proving their independence and power, nagging, retaliating, and so many other games that go on throughout the process of dating and in their relationship. Naturally, this kind of role-playing harms relationships even more than the first kind.

98. Couples like to play certain roles in order to set precedence and enforce their needs. They try to set artificial boundaries and prove their superiority from the beginning. Therefore, it is becoming impossible to sense sincerity and people's personalities. These role-playings (including retaliations or harsh reactions, as their defence mechanisms) are rather justified considering that everybody gets hurt in relationships at some point. Partners play games for both good or evil goals, yet they lose their chances of relaxing and being natural, which could indeed improve their relationship.

99. By playing games, couples have minimized both their own and their partners' objectivity. Thus, they suffer personally, while their relationships follow destructive paths.

100. By role-playing, couples are also losing the opportunity of finding companions who might appreciate them for who they really are. Instead, they only struggle with their own phony personalities (to appear convincing and natural), as well as with their partners' (to know them better perhaps).

101. Nowadays, most people like to rely on their clever Model to play appealing roles for attracting sympathy and love, while also hiding their strong Egos and haughtiness. In new societies where arrogance has found such a strong value, even Model often advocates pomposity. Thus, it is getting difficult to understand who a person really is behind so much show of self-importance.

102. Women are becoming more active socially and placing a high value on living life to its fullest. They need to do more things, go to various functions, and travel extensively. At the same time, men are becoming more passive, content, and couch potatoes, partly due to the declining chances for maintaining good relationships.

103. It is fair to say that women are the stronger gender overall. Men are a weaker gender, due to emotional vulnerability (personality), although women are more emotional. The reasons for this seeming contradiction are fathomable from this book's varied discussions about new gender roles and odd relationship trends. Actually, men's weakness is widely known and readily propagated, nowadays. Even advertising agencies exploit this perception whenever they can benefit from it (see note 119 below). Women are also aware of men's vulnerability. Therefore, it is natural that they often attempt to use this information to push their ideologies and obtain everything they believe they deserve.

104. Due to their higher reliance on intuition, decisiveness, and the teachings of the new culture, women are trying to be in charge of the family. They seem to be good at it, too, in many respects. Yet, in the process, they also feel the need to prove their superiority to men. Well, since women are the

stronger gender in reality, why should not they be in charge or show off their superiority occasionally? The problem is that any type of superiority by either gender cannot work in the new world, where equity, individualism, independence, and satisfying our personal needs are so much emphasized.

105. Thus, women's attempt to prove their superiority leads to further mistrust and deterioration of relationships. Except, of course, in the cases where husbands prefer to be fully passive and/or submissive. In fact, many women try to make their spouses submissive in order to feed their own Egos and ELove. Some women might think, "Why not give it a try, anyway, and see if it works." However, in the end, this situation cannot prevail in progressive relationships.

106. Relationships would go through a lengthy, unpredictable transition period, while women try to assert themselves and find their identity.

107. During this transitional period, women will have difficulty being a modest (content) wife in a social environment that advocates a domineering attitude to enforce equality and identity. Many women have been successful in practising this approach in their relationships already. They present very appealing role models for the rest of them.

108. In fact, women's influence over one another is too strong to be ignored—by either gender. Mothers, daughters, female colleagues and friends are placing lots of pressure on one another, nowadays, to behave assertively. Any woman who attempts to behave outside the new norms may be ousted. More importantly, however, she would feel miserable for not being a typical (assertive) woman like others.

109. It is quite likely that many men have become passive and submissive, since they are less capable of bonding together, thus becoming weaker, too. Moreover, they are less eager to build a strong identity. Their presumed logical minds, passivity, and neediness for a mate are keeping them the

weaker gender they have probably been psychologically and emotionally all along.

110. Men's resort to violence and physical domination are, in fact, good clues about their inability to keep up with the kind of games that women are better at playing so naturally with such high stamina. Men's frustration is also due to their inability to keep up with women's endless needs and demands, which men usually find illogical, anyway.

111. Women appear to be winning most of the battles in their relationships, but it is doubtful that any gender can win the ongoing war. Naturally, as long as one gender is weaker, relationships remain dysfunctional. Not enough respect and challenge make the stronger partner stay in the relationship or take it serious enough. This fact is indeed most relevant in new cultures where individualism and self-esteem have found such high values.

112. Therefore, women's urge to establish their superiority in the new era would not benefit anybody in the long run. Women are behaving naturally, of course, based on their inherent personality strengths and strong bonding capacity. Nonetheless, their efforts are already putting relationships in great jeopardy. They would be (are) the ones suffering the most from the repercussions of the existing situation, as they are more sensitive and they believe in love.

113. Surely, relationships get into trouble because both partners are at fault in some respects. And also because the whole society is losing control over both social and relationship norms. Even when a partner is smart, patient, and humble to make the relationship work, the prospects of saving his/her relationship is still gloomy. The reason is that his/her modest behaviour is viewed as a sign of weakness, instead of goodness. He/she is treated poorly or ignored. So both partners are normally forced to be assertive, which usually turns into aggressiveness and quarrels.

114. Ironically, the situation with relationships now resembles the global warming mayhem. Nobody is keen to accept the existence of a fundamental problem or do anything about it. The main reason, also like global warming, is mainly the economy. Materialism and hypocrisy do not allow partners to become more realistic about the lifestyles, mentalities, and values overwhelming their integrity.

115. Women go into their next relationships with even higher expectations instead of less. They believe that their reasons for leaving their past relationships (e.g., need for more love or compassion) had been justified, thus their next marriage must make up for everything they had missed before. They want to prove to themselves and others that abandoning their past relationships had been a right decision. Therefore, they look for more love, luxury, and security. Conversely, men usually prepare themselves for less authority and set lower expectations if they decide to get into another serious relationship.

116. An effect of women's intuitiveness is that their priorities change a lot after bearing children. For one thing, they feel obliged to exercise lots of authority to make their children follow their rules. A mother's innate urge to manage her and her children's lives makes her authoritative, commanding, and demanding. These mostly instinctual urges erupt when her life begins to get hectic with children, and sometimes a lazy husband, testing her patience. She also finds less time for her husband after children are born. Thus, he is given a lower priority and importance, maybe not intentionally but rather practically. Moreover, she learns eventually that it is more efficient and natural to treat her husband like another one of her children. She must get things organized and done quickly and decisively the way she has found productive thru her child-rearing chores. She now finds these tactics, i.e., commanding, demanding, impatience, and nagging, most natural and effective for running the family affair.

117. For men, however, their wives' gradual (but drastic) change feels unnatural and annoying eventually. They attribute it to their wives' loss of interest and romance. In this setting, women look rather insensitive, impatient, and sometimes even cruel, in the way they manage the whole household, including their husbands.

118. Nevertheless, women's decisiveness goads them to play a stricter role in building relationship settings and imposing the rules. Men, on the other hand, are lazy to argue or fuss too much. Thus, more women are becoming in charge of the family, while men are getting more submissive. Within this relationship atmosphere, most partners, especially men, learn to stay passive in order to cope with their substandard relationship situation and minimize arguments.

119. The existing culture diminishes the zeal for teamwork by stressing on individualism, feminism, rivalry, and winning. Actually, an image of men's submissiveness (and maybe idiocy) is propagated regularly even in TV commercials to sell products to women. For example, while writing about gender differences, a couple of TV commercials caught the author's eyes. They reflect how new social trends regarding relationships are grasped and exploited even by advertisers:

The first commercial was about Multigrain Cheerios. The box apparently refers to 120 calories per serving. The husband makes an innocent comment to his wife: "Are you trying to watch your diet?"

"Do I look like I need to watch my diet?" the wife asks irately with sarcasm.

"No, honey, I'm just stating what the box says (about its low calories)," the poor husband replies with a guilty tone in absolute panic.

"What else the box says?" the wife demands.

"The box says, 'Shut up, Steve.'" the husband replies with shame and misery. The wife smirks.

The second commercial was about McCain's Deep and Delicious frozen cake. The wife is enjoying the cake. And the husband is trying to draw his wife's support about his dream of becoming a mime. However, she is ignoring his comments and miming enactments, while absorbed by the cake's taste. When she notices him finally, she demands with impatience, "What're you doing?"

The husband freezes in his miming gesture like a lamb suddenly facing a lion. "I'm living my dream," he replies with total panic and desperation again. "Stop it," the wife orders him.

The husband remains scared stiff, helpless and mute, as the commercial ends. The wife makes the ruling and that is the end of the story for the poor husband who likes to live his dream of becoming a mime, maybe only as an amateur.

Humour is allegedly the intention of these commercials, to sell their products. However, they are propagating men's passivity and subordination in relationships in the new era —which is largely true but not a proper viewpoint. They exploit the notion of women putting men down regularly and men's inability to do a darn thing about it. They think it is funny! They advocate women's power, all for the sake of flattering and encouraging them to buy their products.

120. These commercials demonstrate the reality of relationships, but also propagate arrogance and ignorance. Our culture appears to find women's superiority funny and acceptable, including aggression towards men. How are we going to convince ourselves that tainting our cultures with shoddy mottos and attitude is ruining our chances for coexistence and gender synergy? How many more centuries before we are convinced? Is a century a good guess?!

121. If someone asks the author to identify the most destructive force damaging relationships and widening gender gap, he would suggest 'Hollywood.' Those fantastic love stories, senseless gender confrontations, and meaningless endings

have been contaminating the brains of the public all over the world. Some ignorant writers are doing a major social disservice by their unrealistic, simple-minded scripts. A scene in the movie *Two Weeks Notice* with Sandra Bullock and Hugh Grant is quite confusing and rude: Late at night, Sandra is returning a pair of shoes she had borrowed from her friend—a weird timing all by itself, *unless as an excuse to pick her friends' brain urgently!* After the friend goes down and opens the door, they sit down near the curb to talk. The friend's husband appears at the window of their apartment, looks down into the street with concern, and asks, "Everything's okay?" The wife yells at him with a smutty tone, "Not now! Everything is not about you!" Her comment and tone of voice has no relevance and meaning in that scene or in the context of the whole movie. It only reflects the absurdity of relationships' atmosphere abused merely for some cheap laughter. "Okay," the humiliated husband mumbles with dismay as he withdraws away from the window. Surely, he would have been accused of apathy if he had not tried to ensure his wife was okay, because all he knew was that she had gone downstairs to answer the door that late at night.

122. Women's higher intuition makes them hasty and adamant in their judgments and raises their tendency to see and feel things without exchanging information. Often they believe they can read their husbands' minds and detect the hidden clues in their eyes or conversations. They also assume that their husbands have the same level of intuition to grasp their wishes without communicating all the points to them clearly. They say something and expect their husbands to read between the lines and grasp their intentions. Then, they get surprised and frustrated when their husbands do not comprehend their messages. Often they believe that their husbands have gotten the message, but are merely refusing to accept it or do something about it. Women believe that

men are (or should be) as careful and intuitive as women are. They do not recognize that men's lower intuitiveness cannot be helped. Furthermore, men's *crude urge for logic* dictates their need for clear communication, instead of guessing the meaning of a vague message.

123. Overall, women usually do not steer, if not resist, an open and precise communication, maybe because they feel their husbands are not listening or interested, anyway. However, women have also become oversensitive and react harshly when men cannot understand their ambiguous messages. As noted above, women's intuition is often filling the gap that apparently hinders men's grasp of a message without full communication. Men require clarity and women resist it, since they find it unnecessary and unromantic, or they stay vague merely out of spite occasionally as well. They simply expect their husbands to grasp their meanings and needs. For example, a husband complained to the author that whenever his wife realized her mistake, she only tried to make up for it by preparing his favourite meal, buying him a pair of socks, or making some kind of an indirect gesture of these natures. However, she never apologized directly or admitted that she had made a mistake. She just expected to get the matter resolved (swept under the rug) without acknowledging the problem or discussing it. He said that, without an open discussion regarding the problem and a sincere apology, the matter never got resolved in his mind and his wounds never healed. Actually, he considered his wife's behaviour (the gestures of buying him a present or cooking a fine meal) another type of manipulation and her rising arrogance.

124. Couples usually miscalculate the hurdles of finding a new companion and building a new home with another partner after leaving the existing one. They are usually naïve and optimistic about their chances of finding a sensible match, even in their older ages. This is especially true for women

who are looking for men of higher qualities after their past relationships fail. Thus, couples' problems and frustrations might keep growing in their second and third relationships. On the other hand, many people learn to resign and admit that their best option is to stick it out after realizing the depth and prevalence of relationship obstacles, nowadays. They just become rather passive in their relationships.

125. Many smart couples prefer to face their relationships' flaws more realistically, as they get used to its shortfalls and their partners' idiosyncrasies after many years of sharing both memories and life's hardships together. They learn to live with their relationship flaws by always recalling its merits. They admit that both partners in almost all relationships are most likely annoyed by each other's quirks. They know that tolerating the imperfections of their existing relationship is easier than learning about, and accepting, the new flaws of a stranger (a new companion) all of a sudden. In particular, men are also lazy to go through the hassle of finding a new companion if the existing relationship is not too bad.
126. People usually expect peace in a new relationship after bearing their previous partners' flaws. For men, especially, staying lonely seems preferable to living with a person who usually brings different kinds of idiosyncrasies and childish demands. People abhor learning new stuff and adjusting, especially at the later stages of their lives. With old age, they need less sex, thus have less patience or incentives, anyway, while getting more grouchy and demanding, too.
127. We look for companions to relieve our loneliness, but soon realize the absurdity of our dreams and efforts, since most relationships actually make us feel the ultimate depth of loneliness and helplessness.
128. Everybody, especially women, is getting more sensitive and defensive in their interactions with others because of their gloomy experiences, growing gender differences, and the growing aggressiveness in society. Certainly, this trend stirs

more psychological pressures in relationships. We talk with people and our partners with apprehension (superficially), to avoid triggering their Egos and starting an argument. This situation keeps relationships too unnatural and edgy. Meanwhile, people are also getting more aggressive and offensive in response to their partners' assertiveness; as the saying goes: the best defence is offence.

129. Relationships get into trouble when partners are unhappy with themselves and their lives. Thus, they depress each other with their harsh attitudes, too. Often they blame their partners for their own gloom, boredom, career failures, or unfulfilled dreams. Sometimes they nag at each other just to conceal their own shortfalls, for example, in socializing. Then, they gradually hate each other, because they believe their partner is actually responsible for their unhappiness. Does this attitude apply more to one gender?!

130. Partners waste a lot of time and energy on faultfinding and blaming each other in hopes of improving their relationship!

131. However, couples can help their relationships only if they realize that, in the end, it does not matter whose fault the problems are as long as those issues remain irreconcilable.

132. The bottomline is that couples must either find mutually agreeable solutions (a suitable relationship model) to relate somehow, or separate. When relationship problems grow, the best solution is to find ways of relating (living together) somewhat passively at a lower level of the relationship tree (model). Struggling to solve relationship problems per se is usually futile due to partners' irreversible idiosyncrasies. Sadly, we humans have proven that not even our logic and love can help us solve our personal or social (including economic and political) problems.

133. Gender struggles to reach some illusory balance of power and equality is continuing at many levels, and the situation would most likely get out of hand in the future, with global destructive outcomes.

134. What works for women in a relationship does not work for men anymore, and vice versa. Especially, men and women mistrust the opposite genders much more than their own.

135. Actually, it appears we are reaching an era where men can no longer be what women want (in terms of character) and vice versa. *Should we wonder, ironically, if the increasing same-sex relationships are partly due to the same gender's abilities to get along better?*

136. We have difficulty learning from our mistakes and from the pains that our relationships are causing us. We prefer to suffer and hurt one another than change our views about the inherent limitations of relationships, particularly within the existing lifestyles. Accordingly, it would be hard for the radical messages of this book to find popularity amidst the mass of beautifully sorted messages (and social values) promising prosperity, love, and happiness to everybody.

137. One of the main goals of a relationship framework is to bring *objectivity* back into rélationships. However, a main hurdle is selling the idea of objectivity to women who are used to dealing with issues intuitively, and to men whose sense of logic has already made them dogmatic.

138. Nonetheless, society must gradually propagate some basic guidelines of a relationship framework. A more practical atmosphere should replace gender struggles for superiority. Finding a balance of power and valid identities for genders requires some form of objectivity eventually. Otherwise, chaos will bring family relationships to a halt.

139. A puzzling point is, 'What kinds of partners are couples looking for when they insist on breaking each other's pride, mainly by competing with each other so relentlessly?' In particular, a relevant question is, "Whether women can ever find submissive men attractive and trustworthy at all?" How could women enjoy or respect weak men?

140. Another major conflict is emerging: Couples expect their partners to be strong, competitive, and assertive outside the

house to maximize families' welfare, but be submissive and passive at home to accommodate them.

141. The emerging trends in society, especially couples' needs for individuality and independence, are irreversible. And people's psychological attributes cannot be changed, either. Thus, the only solution for our relationships is to find new mechanisms and relationship principles to match our new needs.

142. In addition, couples must get more serious about modifying their mindsets and viewing relationships in a progressive perspective. They should do so for increasing their chances of building reliable relationships.

143. Partners' obsession for individualism puts more distance between them if they do not understand the necessity of choosing a proper relationship model together and staying tactful and mindful of their relationship's unique needs and limitations. Working within a fair, solid framework, while advocating partners' independence, rectifies this problem a lot. Couples learn to respect and bear their partners' need for independence as a major facet of teamwork. Meanwhile, finer teamwork mechanisms should be developed, too.

144. The way we behave nowadays, hardly can we find our soul mates. Even if we happen to find them by accident, we just keep losing them because of our phony personalities and ideologies, not to mention our idiotic games and Egos. It is interesting that even couples with similar values, lifestyle, and priorities keep rejecting one another, since they do not give themselves a chance to relate authentically and choose a proper relationship model.

145. Some people indeed find their soul mates, but lose them soon when their own oversensitivity gives them erroneous impressions about the health of their relationships and the purpose of relationships in general. They lose their partners due to their fantasies, about love, individualism, money, a better life with a different partner, etc. High expectations

and idiotic misperceptions are making couples lose the soul mates they have already found.

146. Partners get too intimate too early in hopes of showing their love, trust, and loyalty, instead of proving all of these high qualities gradually thru their actions and right attitude. Often, partners actually try to manipulate each other by showing off a polished image of themselves. Nevertheless, statistics show that most couples end up losing their love, trust, and loyalty in their relationships.
147. Partners try to exploit each other (cleverly or intuitively) by *activating their MLove to fake SLove to fulfil their ELove.*
148. People assume they are (or can be) loving, trustworthy, or loyal. Yet, all evidences indicate that humans are impure by nature, then environment makes them even more cruel and aggressive.
149. Relationships suffer from humans' natural defects more than anything else, while gender differences exacerbate the problems. Some artificial expressions of passion, as a result of attraction or other needs of partners, do not change their true nature as humans with all their inherent defects and all kinds of gender quarrels.
150. Our rampant relationship issues are causing more mistrust amongst the youths. Thus, each generation is causing more damages for the relationships of the future generations. We are making our children more sceptical about marriage and less prepared to deal with its requirements, especially its most likely consequence, i.e., separation.
151. Accordingly, gender differences and quarrels are causing more cynicism for every generation about the opposite sex.
152. Driven by the recent popular ideologies, including positive thinking slogans, people like to believe that life is beautiful and that happiness is within reach. Yet, most prominent philosophies and our personal experiences indicate just the opposite: That life is nothing but a place for suffering and paying for our past or present sins. The point is that our

idealism and search for this phantom happiness are farce and misleading many couples; they put too much demand on each other recklessly before finally separate.

153. Many philosophers suggest that existence cannot be a happy affair, because the minute we have nothing to do, and can supposedly enjoy life, we get bored. Thus, we look for adventure, work, or a new companion to rejuvenate our lives. However, they all make us suffer, too, especially our relationships.

154. It is a pity that our misguided perceptions about love and happiness prevent us from taking advantage of our only opportunity to suffer less in this world: That is, by bringing more objectivity into our relationships and enjoying one another, instead of arguing about our superficial needs and obsessions, especially this illusive 'happiness.' We are just proving philosophers right, in fact, about life being merely a place for suffering. Ironically, we suffer most from our relationships (or lack of them) due to our own immature expectations and games.

155. Being optimistic and positive about life are useful tools. However, when they cause gross misperceptions and raise our naïve expectations, e.g., for love or a better partner, they should be construed as another factor for partners' confusion and relationship failures.

156. The bottomline is that if positive thinking and 'living in the now' schemes worked, everybody would have benefited from these magical cures by now and we could see all those happy faces around us. Relationship issues would have disappeared and everybody would have been living happily with their soul mates. Instead, all we see is more depressions, addictions, unrealistic expectations, suicides, neediness, personal failures, divorces, despair, and self-pity, nowadays. Antidepressants are the highest used drug now (in the U.S. in particular) to help people continue living and suffering.

157. Many people are edgy these days, because their positive thinking alone, even when they combine it with a great deal of personal efforts, does not seem to help them. They still lose their companions to the phony life philosophies that are misleading people, and they lose their life savings in financial markets due to other people's gimmicks, greed, or incompetence.

158. Still, we struggle all our lives to find something creative to do or a worthy companion to give us some moments of happiness. Some spiritualists, of course, believe that we could help ourselves a little if we learned to be a better human being and stayed content, which is a tough mission for most of us.

159. Nowadays, being a good human does not always pay off, anyway. He/she is often perceived as a weak and passive individual and not taken seriously. It may not help (actually damage) his/her relationship, anyway, if his/her partner is not an equally good human being. Therefore, being a good person might not be necessarily useful for drawing other people's compassion or achieving tangible benefits.

160. The only benefit of being good is to mitigate our suffering and possibly get a better chance to relate to our partners unselfishly. This is a grand incentive, though, if we learn to be a bit wiser.

161. Along with our personal efforts to become a better human and partner, we should consider a wide range of radical changes in our mentalities as well as social setting to make our relationships more constructive.

Epilogue

Gender differences have become more vivid and prevalent in the new era and they will continue to be responsible for a big portion of relationship conflicts. In fact, partners' struggles to establish their gender identities and balance their needs for dependence and independence would lead to further alienation, inner conflicts, and stress for spouses. Their abilities to relate and cooperate would diminish, as life burdens, relationships' ambiguities, and personal quirks (noted all along) grow, while gender differences and genders' search for their identities keep making marriages more complex and unmanageable as well. Couples get more confused about relationship purposes every day and feel more frustrated and helpless to relate emotionally, effectively, and efficiently.

These vile, depressing trends will get more out of control in future decades, unless couples change their mentalities about the purposes and potentials of relationships and align their personal needs and expectations accordingly by abandoning their naïve needs. It is also vital for scholars and governments to find practical solutions urgently to revamp the existing laws that are actually escalating gender conflicts, thus contributing to the demise of marriages and societies.

As a major step, people and society must realize and work on the **six fundamental facts** mentioned on pages 14-15 and summarized below about gender qualities and quirks:

1. Gender differences are blessings if viewed and tackled wisely.
2. People's common quirks cause even more marital frictions than their differences.
3. People's quirks and qualities are deeply interwoven within their unchangeable personalities.
4. Rather than emphasizing on, and bragging about, genders' unique identities, partners should learn compromise and teamwork.
5. People, societies, and governments should revamp their mentalities and approaches with regard to the purposes and potentials of relationships.
6. In particular, people and society should stress on genders' unique qualities and differences for increasing teamwork and synergy in society and families, instead of pushing raw ideals about individualism and equality.

If couples were not so adamant (needy) about controlling their partners, and if people stopped encouraging one another to seek perfect relationships and love, they could enjoy many big advantages of relationships. Alas, our hang-ups about some juvenile ideals such as individualism and equality have ruined our capacities for teamwork and compassion. Sadly, our crude obsessions for love, happiness, objects, power, and prestige hinder the chance of enjoying our relationships and lives. Both genders are responsible for some aspects of these shortfalls in some ways and we all suffer at the end.

References

List of References

The following main concepts and terms used in this book are explained further or quoted in this section merely for scholars' review and interested readers' ease of reference.

Love Definitions

The following definitions distinguish three types of love noted in this book. Other books by this author in these series provide more details about this topic.

- SLove (selfless love) is the purest kind of love we usually feel towards our children, Nature, and possibly our artistic creations. With SLove, we Serve (give) love Selflessly without expecting to get love in return. Thus, prefix 'S' could also stand for 'Serving.'
- ELove (egotistic love) reflects the selfish need for love and attention and is mostly a reflection of insecurity. With ELove, people demand (Expect) love egotistically. Thus, 'E' could also stand for 'Expecting.'
- MLove (model love) is the tactful expressions of love to show compassion and social etiquette. With MLove, we try to Moderate our relationships Modestly with our tactful Model. Thus, 'M' could also stand for 'Moderating.'

Definitions of Four Personality Factors

The following four personality factors reflect people's major urges to go around and do the things they do.

- **Instincts** drive many of our urges starting from the basic urge for sex up to the complex urge for spirituality. This factor reflects the *inner self* of a person.
- **Model** drives our urges to socialize and adapt. This factor reflects the *social orientation* of a person and his/her need for acceptance.
- **Ego** drives our urges to defend ourselves and impose our desires on others. Ego reflects the *object orientation* of a person, mainly greed and a need to succeed in acquiring objects or dominating people.

- **Logic** drives our urges for decision making and planning. It reflects our ability to use our brain and the strength of our cognition. This factor reflects the *goal orientation* of a person.

Personality Chart and Ratings

The history of personality factors and ratings suggested in this book goes back a few decades to the time I was working on my Ph.D. in California and contemplating my dissertation. The hypotheses, design, and testing procedures were in place within a few months. A questionnaire was also developed for collecting information from the public, including the large population on the campus. Volunteers were asked to fill out a three-page questionnaire or sit for a fifteen-minute interview.

A preliminary study of the results, based on inputs from over hundred-fifty subjects, proved interesting and useful for many new purposes, but not quite for the original objective of gauging people's personality factors. It became apparent that subjects had become too over-conscious to reveal anything truthful regarding their personalities. This was equally true for both interviews and questionnaires. In fact, it appeared that the information the subjects provided was indeed contrary to (if not the exact opposite of) what it would have been if their brains could be read directly or they were connected to a lie detector. Everybody seemed eager to prove being a different person. Besides learning a lot about humans' behaviour, my intuition and curiosity grew for reading between the lines that people offered cleverly through the questionnaire or interview.

In fact, it is rather easy for almost everybody to detect and measure other people's Model (a bizarre mix of flexibility and showiness) and Ego (a mix of doggedness and haughtiness). Instincts and Logic are hard to detect and measure directly, but they can be estimated indirectly based on people's ratings for Model and Ego. That is, my subsequent studies have shown that the rating for Instincts is normally a complement of Ego's rating. For example, if we rate a person's Ego at say 85 out of 100 max, his rating for Instincts would be 15. Similarly, the rating for Logic complements the rating for Model. Therefore, if the rating for Model was, let us say, 65, his rating for Logic would be 35. All these ratings are mostly subjective, yet they provide good data for drawing general conclusions about the way one's personality operates. We can use several criteria to arrive at Model and Ego ratings for a person, which avail the ratings for his Instincts and Logic as well. We can then make some final refinements if necessary based on other information and criteria applicable to that person.

The above hypotheses about the complementary nature of each pair of 'Ego and Instincts' and 'Model and Logic' have jumped up and become plausible from the results of the initial survey. It makes sense somewhat that the more we use our Ego, the more we dampen our instinctual urges and intuition. Equally reasonable is the assumption that human Logic is compromised faster (and we become more reckless), the more we get obsessed with adaptation and being accepted in society at any cost—perhaps even losing our integrity. Nevertheless, the inherent interconnectivity of the four personality factors is intriguing, while hopefully more proofs and explanations for these hypotheses become available in the future.

Obviously, I could not justify my rather crude, subjective methodology for rating subjects' personality factors. It surely could not qualify for writing a scientific paper or dissertation, especially because many of my deductions contradicted the subjects' official answers. This is probably a valuable lesson any social scientist or human behaviour scholar learns: That with so little control over subjects' responses, we usually get unreliable data. We can make our questions as indirect and innovative as possible in hopes of distracting the subjects' minds from our intentions. Still, people read between the lines and react even more creatively in their own ways. Overall, it seemed that neither my subjective assessments of subjects' personality, nor their direct responses could satisfy the validity and reliability requirements of the conclusions offered in my dissertation.

Therefore, I choose a more mathematical dissertation topic to avoid the need for human input. In a sense, I gave up on the chance of reaching the depth of people's psyches and getting truthful data required for scientific assertions. At the same time, I was drawn to this odd personality model even more after facing people's natural resistance to be sincere even with themselves. Rather than discarding my pet project entirely, gauging humans' personalities remained a rather curious habit for me all along.

Everybody is keen intuitively to judge every person s/he knows or meets even if it is only for ten minutes. I have been doing the same thing in the last thirty years, albeit a bit more scientifically, based on certain criteria developed early on and refined further through experience and analyses. This informal interest to rate friends, family members, colleagues, strangers, and the public, through simple interactions or during seminars and therapies has provided unscientific records of personality ratings of others, up to five subjects per month. Some people might have been rated 2-5 times over the years in different life circumstances along various behavioural elements, e.g., their decisiveness level. This secondary information has been useful for various purposes, including the gender distinctions noted for the Gender Qualities and Symptoms.

The above general background provides an insight about the source of the personality ratings used in this and my other books. The simplified Personality Chart depicted below shows how four personality factors work together in order to present a person to others and in the society. A more elaborate chart and discussions about this topic are available in *The Nature of Love and Relationships* and a new book devoted to human personality will be released later, hopefully.

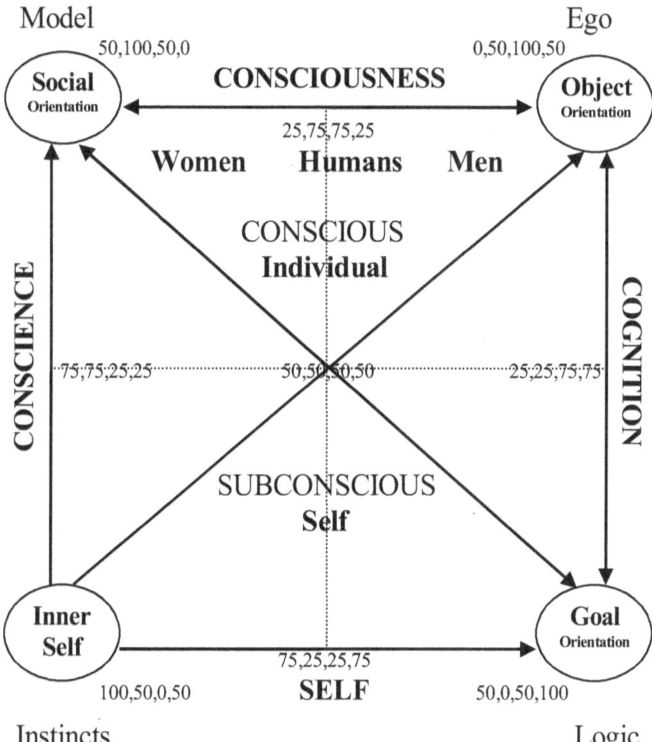

The upper part of the Chart shows the open side of human personality, the 'Conscious Individual.' The Model and Ego factors of our personality help us portray our individuality and identity consciously.

The lower part of the Chart shows the 'Subconscious Self,' which is largely the hidden aspect of human personality. Our instincts and logic are inner urges that drive us to live and do things intuitively, most often without being conscious of how they (instincts and logic) are operating within us. Sometimes, we are aware and pay attention to our instincts and logic. This indicates that accessing our 'unconscious self' is not out of our reach totally. It simply requires meditation and self-awareness.

The point shown as 'Humans' at the top of the Chart offers an approximate rating for human personality. This rating means that an average human in modern society is only slightly driven by instincts (about 20% of all his/her instinctual capacities), s/he knows how to adapt to his/her environment by using his Model (on about 70% of occasions), s/he is highly self-centred and object-oriented (in about 80% of his/ her dealings with people), and s/he applies logic somewhat (about 30% of his/her full potential). This rating is obviously too far off the ideal personality imaginable for a relatively good personality. Thus, using the above noted percentages, we can estimate humans' personality rating as (20,70,80,30). It shows their application of their instincts, model, ego, and logic respectively.

Exploring the data a bit deeper, men and women with all types of personality ratings could be found anywhere on the Chart. However, it appears rather safe to suggest the average ratings of (30,80,70,20) and (10,60,90,40) for women and men respectively, as shown in the Chart as 'Women' and 'Men'.

An *imaginary* perfect human might be able to use 100% of every four factors and attain the highest levels of efficiency, effectiveness, and emotional capacity. In that bizarre society, human rating would be (100,100,100,100). Therefore, we can theoretically say that a super human could possibly earn 400 points, one point for every percent of personality factors. At the present time, it seems that people living in modern cultures get at best a total of 200 points, while the variations along their four personality factors remain drastically unbalanced and problematic. Humans can never reach 400, but even getting to 250 would be a big accomplishment provided a better balance among the four factors is created as well. Realistically, though, we may expect the score for a socially fit and balanced person to be (50,50,50,50). This score presents a plausible personality since the four personality factors remain complementary. This is plausible more theoretically as well.

Other Uses of the Personality Chart

1. The arrows in the Personality Chart suggest that:
   - Our instincts drive us to develop our personality factors Model, Ego and Logic, which represent humans' 'social, object, and goal' orientations respectively.
   - Our Model, Ego, and Logic interact amongst themselves constantly to set up a person's mental orientation at any specific moment, though everybody has a rather unique, consistent personality orientation overall, e.g., in terms of his/her egotism, sociability, and objectivity.
   - The plausible innate connectivity between Instincts and Ego as well as between Model and Logic (as shown by diagonal arrows in the chart) seem quite intriguing and in need of more research beyond the author's elementary hypotheses offered in this book—with respect to their probable complementary relationships.
2. The above personality chart can help for developing:
   a) Various tests for measuring each person's personality along the dimensions specified in the Chart.
   b) A standard for the 'balanced personality' only for the sake of making comparisons possible.
   c) Rules and principles about the ways personality ratings of individuals relate to their behaviours in relationships.
   d) Average rating for a common person.
   e) Rules and principles about personality compatibilities for maximizing the effectiveness of marital relationships.
   f) A rating for a normal person, who has the highest chance of relating effectively in his/her relationships. Most likely a relationship becomes successful if the couple has high personality (balanced) ratings, i.e., close to (50,50,50,50). However, it is interesting to develop theories about the chance of other kinds of complementary or contradictory personalities being able to get along effectively within a particular relationship model.

A Recap of Personality Factors

The following diagram simply provides a collection of all the points made about gender differences in Part I of this book.

Genders Qualities and Symptoms

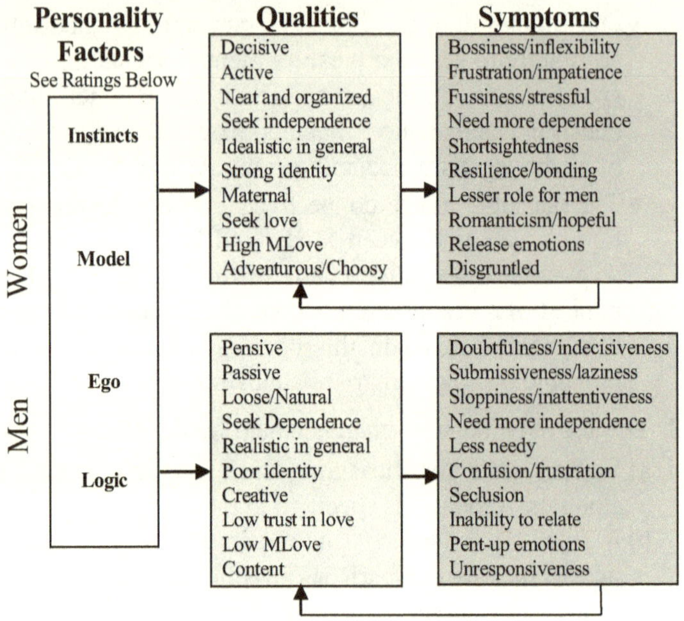

Thus, the following personality ratings:

Personality Factors	Women	Men	Humans
Instincts	30%	10%	20%
Model	80%	60%	70%
Ego	70%	90%	80%
Logic	20%	40%	30%
Total Points	**200**	**200**	**200**

Sample Personality Ratings

A large number of personality ratings have been accumulated from various sources and settings informally by the author in previous decades, especially the last ten years. A set of criteria has been applied to estimate each personality rating, but the total score (for four ratings) is forced to 200 points. The author is planning to prepare a simple methodology for the public to estimate their own or other people's personality ratings easily. Just to provide an insight and some examples, the personality ratings of eight familiar politicians are offered below. These ratings are based on their public speeches, demeanour, deemed honesty, and decisions about citizens' welfare.

	Instincts	Model	Ego	Logic
Stephen Harper:	(10,	85,	90,	15)
Thomas Mulcair:	(20,	75,	80,	25)
Justine Trudeau:	(30,	60,	70,	40)
Elizabeth May:	(40,	80,	60,	20)
Pierre Trudeau:	(20,	65,	80,	35)
John F. Kennedy:	(25,	60,	75,	40)
Rachel Notley:	(25,	75,	75,	25)
Barack Obama:	(35,	65,	65,	35)

The last two individuals on the list were chosen from the author's personality ratings' archive as good candidates with better-balanced personality factors for the present era. They are also exceptional in the way their ratings are significantly different from their genders'. It is also interesting that Justine Trudeau and Rachel Notley have received rather good ratings, despite the author's major apprehension about their persistency to build a huge pipeline to carry oil from Alberta to British Columbia. This is a big environmental concern for the author and people in Vancouver.

You could make your own objective ratings about these authorities or other individuals by following the methodology explained before. That is, estimate Model and Ego first, and then calculate the complementary ratings for Instincts and Logic—100 points for each pair. You can also compare these politicians' ratings with the above average ratings for humans and two genders, as estimated by the author so far.

Human Needs for Dependence and Independence

Humans' conflicting needs for dependence and independence play a major role in developing their personalities and cause so many gender clashes and divorces, nowadays. Accordingly, this topic has been discussed in the main body of the book a lot. Still, the following details seem useful as well for couples who are truly keen in building a functional relationship model for themselves.

We face many inner conflicts while trying to develop our character. They make us think and behave in bizarre ways. We learn how to deal with many of these conflicts eventually and some of them become irrelevant when we move on to the next stages of our lives. However, one particular conflict stays with us for the rest of our lives. This persistent conflict arises when our two fundamental needs for dependence and independence keep clashing constantly in our minds. These inherent needs play a major role in our lives, sometimes more prominently than any single need that humans usually have. In fact, any one of our needs often remains at the mercy of our needs for dependence and independence. Our general needs are often reinforced or dampened only based on our prominent need for independence (or dependence) regardless of the consequences. For example, our pride (a symptom of independence) often defies any single need, even the need for food or survival. We go on hunger strike, sometimes, when pride gets urgency even ahead of our basic needs.

On the other hand, our need for dependence, e.g., the need for passion and a companion, might supersede our need for food or even breathing. We may prefer to die when loneliness is crippling our existence and mind. The point of interest here is that our personal needs for dependence and independence are overwhelming and they cause deep inner conflicts for us personally. Yet, more importantly, partners' inner conflicts due to these needs infect their relationship severely. In particular, the new social setting is affecting genders differently in terms of their needs for dependence and independence as discussed in Chapter Seven and Part I. Anyway, by grasping the intricacy of these needs, we might learn to relate to our partners better. We should realize that both partners' drives for the same needs (especially dependence and independence) should somehow coincide or we just keep widening the gender gap in terms of gender mentalities and abilities to relate.

At adolescence, we get ready to gain our independence from family and their lifestyle. We begin to develop our own thoughts and preferences. We strive to show off our freedom and individualism through all types of rebellions and radical expressions with our opinions, appearance, attire, arts, etc. Meanwhile, a subtle need for dependence creeps into our heads sneakily. We feel the need to belong to groups of friends and family, find a lover, be accepted, and fit within many features of social living (not to mention a foolish sense of need for drugs, alcohol, and cigarettes to feel normal and alive). As we go through life, the number of dependencies piles up in line with our addictions to so many other superficial needs, while we also strive to establish our independence and identity. We get anxious when our independence is constantly threatened by our innate need for dependence on other people and society. Then, ironically, we begin to hate (subtly and subconsciously again) our feelings of dependence and those who seems to be the sources of it, e.g., our parents or spouses, as they seem to be sabotaging our need for independence now.

The contentious issues concerning our personal needs for both dependence and independence are overwhelming, but a list of the main facts is offered on Page 182.

When we get the opportunity of entering a relationship, we recognize the need to give up some of our autonomy for the benefits of companionship. We find this trade-off equitable initially. However, we soon find it humiliating when even small conflicts make us doubt our identity, the purpose of our relationships, and the value of our sacrifices. We hate the way our partner is squashing our independence. The longer we stay in a relationship, the larger the level of inner conflicts between dependence and independence gets, and the more pressure is put on the relationship and us.

Especially, with the social emphasis on individualism and independence, nowadays, our inner conflict due to our needs for dependence and independence has become too prominent. We try to create some level of balance between our needs for dependence and independence in order to make our marriages manageable in societies that are now satiated with slogans of personal identity and individualism. Creating and maintaining this balance is tough, even if such a balance could be found. Most couples have difficulty in this area.

Yet, a deep inner conflict grows in many people's psyches as they seek dependence obsessively due to their prominent insecurities and urgent need for a companion. 'Need for a companion' is a strong, complex personal need that expands across all levels of human needs. Companionship satisfies our basic, medium, and high level needs. Most people look for compassion and a companion almost more than anything else. Although we acknowledge the need for creating a practical balance between independence and dependence, we might be a very needy person inherently. We may prefer to rely totally on our partners. We want to depend on her/him to provide the compassion and passion that we crave. We might even need someone to lead us through life. This is a much higher level of dependence than a normal person's primitive, natural needs for dependence and independence. Meanwhile, we do not want to reveal our neediness to our partner, especially if s/he is not as needy as we are. Thus, while one partner insists on creating a workable balance for partners' independence, the other partner hides his/her need for more (or total) dependence. Yet, he/she hopes all along that his/her obsessive (but unexpressed) need for dependence is understood. Another way of stating this condition is that most individuals' need for ELove has grown irrationally in recent decades, but they hate to admit it. Their Egos stop them from expressing their need for all that extra attention and love, mostly because it is unfashionable to show their vulnerabilities and inability to be independent.

Conversely, some people (especially men) inherently need more independence, but try to hide it to minimize relationship clashes. They build and bear a great deal of inner conflicts, too, which lead to relationship quarrels and hardships. Yet, this group is quite small compared with the large population obsessed for dependence, nowadays.

Overall, even a moderate drive for independence requires (and leads to) a lot of isolation and self-reliance, which only few can manage realistically. Dependence, on the other hand, is mostly synonymous with the need for compassion and a willingness to pay a price for it. We all value compassion a lot. We feel the need for dependence on another individual and society, as we doubt our abilities to survive as independent persons. Some of us need dependency to another person—a lover perhaps—more urgently in order to validate our identity and existence. Yet, our partners and society do not have the capacity to cope with our need for dependence. In most cases, they actually ridicule and take advantage of our perceived weakness, i.e., our inability to be *(or appear)* independent. However, even for people seeking dependence obsessively, their need for independence emerges quite regularly, too. Even this group's need for dependence is not absolute or permanent. It continues to remain an unmanageable urge.

The matter gets fully out of hand when we pretend to be more independent than we really feel we are, or can handle. We are trained, nowadays, to insist on our individuality and independence. That is how we believe we can assert ourselves and show our identity. We learn to play all kinds of roles and games to prove our independence and identity. However, as we engage in these types of silly exaggerations, to prove our independence, we place a higher pressure on our psyches to impose a fake balance between our needs for dependence and independence. We lose touch with reality and our true needs. We are in effect imposing another set of artificial needs on ourselves that are unachievable, thus causing ourselves more inner conflicts and psychological damages. These artificial needs are also widening the gender gap and leading to futile clashes with our partners. At the same time, we are depriving ourselves from fulfilling our need for dependence. We become aggressive in order to show assertiveness, mostly because we do not know the delicate art of assertiveness. Assertiveness might not even be in our nature, anyway. We are fighting our own natural urges to become somebody else. We play the role of an independent person with some imaginary identity, but unfulfilled. This kind of confusion causes identity crisis, of course, and often we feel this deficiency ourselves, too. Yet, we keep seeking more independence, anyway, because we are brainwashed to play those roles; to fight for our individuality and identity no matter what. Our artificial need to show off our independence, as a symbol of freedom and identity, has in fact become quite counterproductive for both our individuality and relationships.

Conversely, many people have become too submissive and dependent upon their relationships. They accept all kinds of humiliations and intimidation, including their partners' deceit and infidelity. Only a few decades ago, infidelity was a taboo and led to an automatic divorce. Not anymore! Yet, even these people, with high dependence orientation and a submissive attitude, have difficulty sustaining their relationships. Their sacrifices go unnoticed and they lose their relationships, too, unexpectedly. Some of these people might eventually learn that it is impossible to depend on others, even their partners. To survive in their relationships without getting hurt too much, they eventually learn to play the role of an independent person with a strong identity. They just have to. They are forced to behave that way, mostly pompously.

The bottomline is that partners' need for dependence is now undervalued vastly at so many levels by new lifestyles, values, personal insecurities, and social pressures. It is trendy to show one's aptitude for individualism. Therefore, people pretend to be independent at big cost to their psyches in order to fit and survive. They are forced into this position (seek independence) to defend themselves and fit as much as possible. However, they remain inherently a dependent, depressed person.

Surely, the smart thing, nowadays, is to not rely on others or their words. They just cannot deliver due to the limitations in their own lives and psyches, and not necessarily out of spite. In fact, beyond people's *instinctual urge* for independence, three other reasons make people struggle for independence: (1) they have become obsessed with their need for expressing individualism and asserting their identity, (2) they must strive to cope with social norms and being accepted, and (3) they eventually learn they cannot rely on others.

Another dependence-independence conflict in relationships happens when partners try to acquire more independence for themselves, but want to maximize their partners' neediness and dependence on them. They strive to gain more power in their relationships by dominating their partners. Therefore, an ongoing struggle continues between partners to maintain a balance of power in order to stop the other from dominating them. Everybody likes more independence for themselves, but much less for their partners. Men were more domineering in the past, but now the trend is reversing fast due to women's struggle to assert themselves more readily. Nonetheless, the power struggle for domination is causing major conflicts in relationships, nowadays. Instead of creating a relaxed setting, partners' quarrels to maintain 'the needed balance' lead to so much more frictions, miscommunications, misperceptions, and mistrust all in itself.

Accordingly, the most destructive trend in society these days has emerged as the result of couples' struggle to cope with their needs for dependence and independence: Some couples seek separation with the slightest inconvenience in their relationships (reflecting high need for independence and individualism); and some couples accept abuse and adultery as they are apprehensive about loneliness and isolation (high need for dependence and compassion). These dire, prevalent extremes show the extent of value changes in new societies. They demonstrate the huge imbalance between our needs for independence and dependence, and a general confusion about the role of marriages as a crucial social concept (requirement). A major conclusion is that we are not as strong as we often wish, or pretend, to be in our dire pretences of independence and individualism. We are unequipped to develop a practical balance between our needs for independence and dependence in our relationships, either. Therefore, the question is whether a framework can be developed and used by couples to align their conflicting urges for independence and dependence in teamwork environments.

The contentious issues concerning our personal needs for both dependence and independence are summarized below:

1. We are not conscious of the complexity and effects of our conflicting needs for dependence and independence. Nor are we aware of the high repercussions of this conflict for us, our relationships, and society in general.

2. We do not know how to define or judge our personal needs for independence and dependence. We do not know how to be independent or dependent, while we strive to satisfy these needs alternately on a regular basis. Some people pretend to be independent and self-reliant when deep down their need for dependence is overwhelming. And some people hurt their identities when they become too dependent and submissive.
3. Since we do not know how to set and maintain a practical balance between our conflicting needs for independence and dependence, we play the kind of roles that society and people suggest, with the highest stress on independence. However, everybody has a different balance of needs for independence and dependence according to his/her unique personality. Ignoring those needs and sticking to a fake balance (and role-playing) stirs confusion and frustration.
4. Partners do not know how to discuss and reconcile their needs for dependence and independence—mostly because it might require some kind of compromise, which they think would be against their identities and independence. Thus, they end up arguing about every detail or decision.
5. Without knowing about our needs for independence and dependence and the suitable balance for us, we expect our partners to behave as if they actually knew what the right balance should be. For example, we want them to respect our independence when we suddenly feel it is time for us to be independent; we ask for a vaster boundary. Then, we expect them to be compassionate and caring as soon as we need their attention to satisfy our need for dependence (ELove).
6. We turn off our partners with our exaggerated shows of independence and self-reliance. And we confuse them and ourselves with our foolish roles and games to enforce our alternating needs for both dependence and independence. These confusing interactions make it hard for partners to

relate to each other peacefully. All along, power struggles to dominate our partners, and push our gender identities, postpone the matter of aligning our needs for dependence and independence. Only arrogance and phoniness prevail in this kind of setting. All these conditions hinder the task of bringing objectivity and peace into marriages. Choosing a proper relationship model also becomes very difficult.

7. As social complexity and the public's intelligence increase every year, people's demands for both independence and dependence will rise. They seek more independence since society pushes them to express themselves and prove their identities more explicitly. However, they also seek more dependence (need for a compassionate companion) due to of the rising level of stress in their daily lives and sense of loneliness. Therefore, people fight more every day with their anxiety and inner conflicts, rather than aligning their needs for independence and dependence.
8. The topics covered in this book show how this increased imbalance (between our needs for both independence and dependence) is forced upon us due to our lifestyles and mentalities. Accordingly, relationships will become more instable in the future and their longevity will continue to decline. Considering this doomed prospect, implementing the 'radical changes' suggested in this author's book, *The Nature of Love and Relationships*, feels crucial and urgent.
9. The inner conflict caused by dependence/independence imbalance affects our moods randomly, usually at worst situations, e.g., when our partner is angry and pushing our nerves. We react harshly, because the presumed balance we had imposed for our independence and dependence needs is threatened. Our partners react harshly, too, for the same reasons—not out of spite perhaps, but only due to chemical and mental reactions in their bodies. This inner conflict seems to be triggered when we get into arguments with our partners. Yet, in reality, it is an ongoing struggle

within us causing all sorts of insecurity and doubts about our identities.

10. A person's needs for dependence and independence are neither complementary nor contradictory. This means that a person's high need for independence (or dependence) does not necessarily imply that s/he has proportionately less need for dependence (or independence).
11. In fact, often a person's needs for both dependence and independence are high or low. This means that, weirdly enough, people's needs for dependence and independence are both opposing and overlapping needs at the same time.
12. Furthermore, many people switch between their needs for dependence and independence regularly and rapidly quite erratically. In such cases, creating a good balance between partners' dependence and independence is even harder. They are usually less-balanced persons to begin with.
13. Each partner's needs for independence and dependence at any moment are quite fluid and fluctuating. This makes the job of balancing each partners' need and demand for the same thing, i.e., dependence or independence, in every instance, very hard. Then, aligning both partners' needs at any instance would become extremely difficult and rarely possible.
14. Despite people's superficial expressions of independence and dependence, they are usually conflicted and confused about these innate, erratic needs prickling their psyches regularly all their lives.
15. Everybody is quite anxious to grasp, gauge, express, and satisfy his/her needs for independence and dependence, but his/her capacity and opportunity for doing all these tasks is very limited.
16. No two partners in a relationship have the same levels of needs for independence and dependence. Thus, agreeing on the sensible degree of independence and dependence for each partner, for choosing a proper relationship model,

and for setting a workable balance in their relationship, becomes too difficult and a contentious issue.

17. For all the above facts, matching two partners' needs and demands for dependence and independence becomes quite cumbersome and controversial.
18. As societies grow and gender struggles for equality and self-realization increase, people's conflicts and confusions about their needs for, and expressions of, dependence and independence would continue to get weirder and more awkward. Accordingly, their quirks and superficial needs would keep increasing as well. This means finding better relationship models and compromising in relationships will become even more difficult and crucial in the years ahead.
19. Accordingly, a great deal of research, contemplation, and education is urgent to find means of giving couples the right tools and mentalities to understand and implement the requirements of building families.
20. The bottomline is that without a direct, serious interest and engagement by governments and scholars to find solutions for marital conflicts, the future of humanity is at even a higher risk, beyond all other threats, if families continue to think and behave the way they are, nowadays.

Meanwhile, to curb their inner conflicts, prospective spouses must somehow deal with their 'dependence vs. independence' needs, both personally and together, in three distinct ways:

1. He/she should first try to establish his/her realistic needs for dependence and independence, based on his/her personality alone, without considering any compromises necessary for being in any serious relationship with a partner. The idea is to establish one's true temperament and needs regardless of social pressures for independence in line with the level of expected compromises needed in a relationship.
2. He/she should figure out the levels of independency and dependency that he/she can envision for his/her partner.

Usually people dislike and avoid partners who seek too much independence. However, more crucial than this case is when a person is unprepared (perhaps psychologically) or unwilling to be responsible for a partner who requires too much dependence (emotionally or financially). Therefore, he/she must gauge his/her potential partner's inclination for dependence/independence realistically before committing him/herself to any partnership.

3. Potential partners should contemplate, establish together, and agree at the outset (before the wedding) regarding the kind of dependency/independency balance they like to have in their relationship, and then choose the right relationship model for them. This balance should coincide with the other two above decisions that each partner must make personally before choosing the right relationship model. The outcome would still never be fully satisfactory, but at least somewhat measured as realistically as possible at the outset before a final decision for marriage is made.

There should be practical tests soon to help spouses with the above three measurements as a supplement to their natural feelings and objective assessments regarding their chances of building a functional family together.

All these precautions seem quite necessary, nowadays, *just to ensure couples know what the heck they are getting into before they express their marital wows with so mush hope and enthusiasm!!*

www.ingramcontent.com/pod-product-compliance
Lightning Source LLC
LaVergne TN
LVHW090943080826
845145LV00003B/872

* 9 7 8 1 9 8 8 3 5 1 0 7 0 *